SpringerBriefs in Anthr

MW01592107

Anthropology and Ethics

For further volumes:
http://www.springer.com/series/11497

Susan Dewey · Tiantian Zheng

Ethical Research with Sex Workers

Anthropological Approaches

 Springer

Susan Dewey
Women and Gender Studies
University of Wyoming
Laramie, WY
USA

Tiantian Zheng
Sociology/Anthropology
State University of New York, Cortland
Cortland, NY
USA

ISSN 2195-0822   ISSN 2195-0830   (electronic)
ISBN 978-1-4614-6491-4   ISBN 978-1-4614-6492-1   (eBook)
DOI 10.1007/978-1-4614-6492-1
Springer New York Heidelberg Dordrecht London

Library of Congress Control Number: 2013932768

Printed on acid-free paper

Springer is part of Springer Science+Business Media (www.springer.com)

For all who are dedicated to advancing knowledge about sex work

Foreword

Dewey and Zheng's *Ethical Research with Sex Workers: Anthropological Approaches*, provides a thoughtful and carefully researched look into the multi-faceted world of sex workers. By drawing from cross-cultural data, the authors describe individuals ranging from destitute street-based and crack cocaine addicted prostitutes to 'high-end' escorts who revel in their upscale way of life. Their extensive analysis avoids the pitfalls of over-simplifying and/or over-generalizing the lives of those employed in the sex industry.

Dewey and Zheng are steadfast in their dedication to understanding the lives and decision-making processes of sex workers. Their desire for truthfulness is accompanied by the empathy and respect they have for each of their informants. They caution fellow researchers against constructing simplistic dichotomized characterizations of sex workers as pure victims or as pure agents. Instead, the authors consider sex workers as multi-layered and multi-positioned individuals who have the right to tell their stories. By doing so, they heed the feminist call to give voice to individuals from all sectors of society.

Dewey and Zheng put forth useful methodologies/protocols for collecting data and for maintaining the privacy of informants. The authors call for the use of a 'Community-Based Participatory Action Research' Model in which sex workers take part in the design and implementation of the investigation, analysis of data, along with the dissemination of findings. Moreover, they provide a number of specific cases where such methodologies/protocols have proven successful.

Dewey and Zheng also document the ongoing debate between advocates of sex worker's rights advocates versus those calling for abolition. In some cases, these heated disagreements have resulted in attacks being made on sex researchers' academic freedom. Sadly, this acrimony has fueled what can be described as anthropology's 'culture of accusation' first documented by Gregor and Gross (2004) and later confirmed by Chacon and Mendoza (2012a, b).

Indeed, the authors describe how the decision to accurately and respectfully report what sex workers tell researchers can come at great personal cost. Sex work researchers have been subjected to unfair accusations from government officials, colleagues, and activists while some family members and friends have shunned them.

An erratum to this Foreword is available at 10.1007/978-1-4614-6492-1_5.

In sum, this work will make great contributions to understanding the different aspects of sex worker research. First, it demonstrates the great socio-economic heterogeneity of this population. Second, it sheds light on the ongoing abolitionist versus sex worker advocacy debate. Third, Dewey and Zheng's methodological contribution will help researchers to collect data in an effective and safe manner. Lastly, this publication exposes many of the ethical dilemmas that anthropologists face when conducting research on sex workers. Therefore, no matter where an investigator stands along the abolitionist/sex worker's rights advocate spectrum, *Ethical Research with Sex Workers: Anthropological Approaches* will serve as a valuable source of insight and information.

Dr. Richard J. Chacon
Series Editor for Anthropology and Ethics
Department of Anthropology
Winthrop University
Rock Hill, SC, USA

Contents

Abstract

This book addresses key ethical challenges faced by anthropologists who study sex work, defined as the exchange of sex or sexualized intimacy for money or something of value. Sex work encompasses a wide range of behaviors and practices that vary significantly in terms of legality, physical contact, social stigma, income, and levels of risk. Each chapter in the book is organized around a central ethical issue that, taken together, provides a comprehensive overview of how researchers address these challenges in their own work and applied practice. Chapter 1 places anthropological engagement with sex work into historical context, including major trends in the literature and trajectories for future research. Chapter 2 discusses ethical issues faced by sex work researchers in the initial stages of research project planning, including the formation of research questions and methodologies that actively seek to reduce the gap between researcher and research subject, research design strategies for minimizing risk and accessing representative samples of sex workers, as well as the utility of engaging in smaller scale ethnographic studies of particular sex worker populations. Chapter 3 assesses the influence of sex work-related legislation and political debates upon researchers' abilities to empirically test assumptions about sex work, and potential difficulties researchers face in obtaining Institutional Review Board approval. Chapter 4, co-authored with the New Orleans and Las Vegas branches of the Sex Workers' Outreach Project (SWOP) describes researchers' strategies for incorporating research participants from research design to the dissemination of findings.

Keywords Sex work • Ethics • Research design • Ethnography • Anthropology

Chapter 1
Anthropological Research with Sex Workers: An Introduction

Susan Dewey

At 4 am on an isolated highway, Kristi turns to me and asks, "Do you mind if I rest my eyes for a minute? I haven't slept for three days." The brilliant red-silver of daybreak is just beginning to cast the snowy fields around us with a shimmering glow as we drive toward another town, where Kristi hopes to retrieve her belongings from a motel notorious for drug and prostitution activity. I have known Kristi for about eight hours, most of which we have spent talking about the tumultuous events she has experienced in the past week. "I'm done," she says, crossing her forearms emphatically as we sat together in the back room of a homeless shelter, "I'm just done." Even at this point in my research on street sex workers' notions of risk, when I feel like I have heard everything, I have to work hard to hold back tears as she tells me about her last few days on the streets, during which was assaulted by her partner, almost raped by a client, and ignored by police officers when she tried to file complaints about both.

"If I can just get my stuff back," Kristi tells me, "I can move on with my life and get clean. I know this shit is gonna kill me."

The shelter director asks me if I can drive Kristi to the motel to get her things from the manager, who is holding them for her. I agree, and we get into my truck at 3 am, as Kristi thinks that she is less likely to run into her abusive partner if we leave early. All is silent and dark as we drive past the shuttered payday loan and pawnshops that populate the strip malls near shelter.

When we arrive at the motel, Kristi is visibly agitated. "They know me real well here," she sighs heavily as she makes her way toward the manager's office door, which is painted green and peeling in places. "She your new caseworker?" the motel manager asks Kristi as he nods toward me, his eyes focused on her from his desk. "Something like that" Kristi says, "she ain't a cop." While I feel awkward at being so conspicuously ignored and easily read as out of place in this environment, I am relieved that, as a small woman, I am not easily mistaken for law enforcement. After a warning that this is the last time he will store her things for her, Kristi and I get on the road, six trash bags loaded with her possessions in the back of my truck.

S. Dewey and T. Zheng, *Ethical Research with Sex Workers*,
SpringerBriefs in Anthropology and Ethics,
DOI: 10.1007/978-1-4614-6492-1_1, © The Author(s) 2013

We have almost left the town limits when she sees a familiar face at a bus stop and shouts, "wait, stop here!" The woman we pull over to greet looks a lot like Kristi, with the ashy skin and blistered lips of a person addicted to crack cocaine. She asks if we are headed back to the city. Kristi looks at me meaningfully, and I can tell that she is judging me, evaluating whether or not I am afraid of her world. I tell myself that I am being unreasonable in my fear of this unknown woman who will only be with us for two hours as we drive back to the city. After that, the anthropologist in me thinks, Kristi will trust me. I tell myself that Kristi and I are building rapport as the woman slides into the backseat, eyeing me with suspicion through the rear-view mirror as she thanks me in a way that seems awkward and profuse.

When we arrive back in the city, we drop the woman off and then unload her things into a storage area near shelter. Kristi is visibly exhausted but gives me a firm and emotional hug before leaving. "Maybe someday you can write a book about my life," she tells me, "I sure got a lot of stories to tell." Her choice of words in expressing her gratitude speaks to both her knowledge of my positionality in the field and, I hope, to some amount of trust. "That would be amazing," I say as we make eye contact, "But let's see where you are in a few months, okay?" I cringe as I hear myself sounding like the social workers I have gotten to know in the past few months; while I respect and like most of them very much, I work hard at carving out a distinct niche as a researcher who can walk in multiple worlds at once. Kristi nods seriously, then closes her door and heads to bed. As I walk back to my truck, I check my phone for the first time in twelve hours and see that my husband, a nice man from down South, has sent me six text messages, the last of which reads, "Are you okay?" It's a question that makes me feel both safe and deeply ashamed of my own privilege.

Six months later in another city, a vice police officer who uses the initials J.T. in lieu of a first name, tells me how he spends his mornings at work searching the Internet for escort advertisements and the later parts of the day driving slowly through areas of the city known for street prostitution in an unmarked car, looking to make arrests. We are sitting in his cave of an office not far from the local jail, a towering monstrosity that at any given time houses a disproportionate number of women of color for prostitution-related crimes. J.T. talks to me about "cleaning up" the streets and "rescuing" women through arrest, explaining that "most of those girls don't really want to be out there. It's just that they think it's the only thing they can do." I can feel his deep sense of pity for the sex workers he arrests, most of whom work on the street and are easier to locate than Internet-based escorts; when I ask him if he thinks that arresting sex workers helps them, he tells me that he has three daughters and looks deeply into my eyes. I think he is trying to tell me that, somewhere deep in his heart, he remains unsure.

The vice police officer does not know that I spent most of the previous day with an escort who spent several hours explaining her strategies for police avoidance as well as the elaborate relationships she engages in with law enforcement. She did not tell me her real name, and I did not ask her to, but she called herself Lucie. In our lengthy conversation, she voiced many of the same beliefs advanced by the sex workers' rights movement since the 1970s: that her body is her own, that sex work gives her the autonomy to earn an income with flexible hours that allow her to pursue creative work, and that she eschews sexual and moral double standards through her work. Still, her descriptions of how stigma has exercised its powerful weight in her life make me wonder, as I did with the vice officer, if Lucie's feelings about work are not a bit more ambivalent. One thing that remains clear, though, is that if one knew that I spoke with the other, our rapport would be broken. I tell myself that as long as I do not reveal any sensitive data in the course of my research and maintain confidentiality in my writing, I am firmly situated on ethical ground. But sometimes, like J.T. and Lucie, I am not so sure.

I chose these ethnographic vignettes after careful consideration of the messages that each might send to readers about sex work. Would I perpetuate enduring popular cultural stereotypes about sex workers as desperate addicts by describing my interactions with Kristi first? Will sex workers' rights advocates feel that I do not demonstrate adequate commitment to their cause when they read about my experiences of walking in multiple worlds with social service providers, law enforcement officers, and sex workers? Worse still, will my researcher colleagues think that I am self-indulgent by choosing to write so openly about my own reactions to these situations? I suppose that only time, and responses to this book, will tell; in the meantime, I have done my best to paint an honest portrait of some of the ethical struggles involved in ethical research across the labor continuum of sex work, which runs the gamut from survival sex workers like Kristi to relatively affluent and highly educated escort women like Lucie.

This book is the result of many years that Tiantian Zheng and I have spent conducting ethnographic field research with sex workers, our conversations with other researchers, and, perhaps most importantly, our deep sense of empathy for the sex worker participants in our research as well as our colleagues who carry out this work with the goal of advancing social justice. We have a total of 25 years' experience carrying out research with sex workers, and this extensive period of time has given us ample opportunity to reflect upon the topics of ethics. Our field sites span a wide range of geographical and cultural areas, and include North-eastern Chinese hostess bars, the anti-trafficking offices of international organizations in Sarajevo, Bosnia-Herzegovina and Yerevan, Armenia, and the rundown strip clubs of the deindustrialized New York State Rust Belt.

Sex work, defined as the exchange of sexual or sexualized intimacy for money or something of value, encompasses a wide range of legal and illegal behaviors that present researchers with a number of socioeconomic, political, and ethical issues. These realities, in turn, potentially complicate scholars' abilities to engage in cutting edge research with potential benefits to sex workers and those who engage in social service or activism with them. We hope that this book will make a small contribution to the sex work-related literature and activist practices by opening a dialogue about the many and varied challenges that this type of research presents. In doing so, we will also endeavor to critically engage with this literature to identify common ethical challenges as well as ways that researchers might engage with sex workers in ethically sound ways.

While anthropologists who study sex work likely all face ethical dilemmas as part of their research, not all have chosen to write about these difficulties. There are a number of reasons for this, including the reality that discussion of ethical dilemmas might be perceived as opening a door to criticism of her (or his) moral principles or standards. It is equally understandable that some anthropologists might prefer to focus their writing energies on their data rather than the ethical struggles they faced in collecting it. Since sex work researchers have not published extensively on these ethical challenges, we have taken a rather novel approach to the issue in the ensuing text. We openly discuss our own ethical struggles and strategies for dealing with them in our respective field sites as well drawing upon the burgeoning literature on sex work to help both novice and experienced sex work researchers critically engage with the topic of ethics.

These constitute timely considerations; in fact, as this book goes to press, the American Anthropological Association is in the process of revising its own Code of Ethics. The most recent version of this Code available at the time of publication notes that anthropological researchers "are members of many different communities, each with its own moral rules or codes of ethics" (AAA 1998). This observation is particularly salient for sex work researchers, who often find themselves positioned at the confluence of many divergent groups that evince an interest in sex work as a social issue, ranging from sex workers themselves to harm-reduction focused outreach workers to abolitionist activists who view all forms of sex work as little more than violence against women.

Sex workers remain as legal and moral criminals in many societies, where they are often positioned as individuals who have transgressed tense boundaries between economic and emotional exchange. This fact in itself opens up a whole range of other possibilities that complicate almost any of the ethical codes that anthropologists might employ in their fieldwork, as the decision to engage with sex work as a subject of research inevitably means entering into hotly contested political and ideological terrain. In the midst of these heated circumstances, our greatest hope is that some of the work presented here will encourage more participatory and community-based research with sex workers as a means toward engaging in collaborative, social justice-driven work that eliminates, inasmuch as possible, the patronizing and cruel distinctions between research and subject.

Anthropological Engagement with Sex Work: A Concise Literature Review

The proliferation of ethnographic research on sex work-related topics in the past two decades has coincided with a more general anthropological interest in sexuality as a topic of inquiry (Donnan and Magowan 2010). This can be seen as an extension of the establishment of feminist theory and modes of inquiry in anthropology from the 1980s onward, when many anthropologists who had begun to pay attention to gender and sexuality as meaningful analytical categories. Many of the first sex work-related publications by anthropologists began to appear in the mid-1990s, and quite a few of these were authored by those who were trained by scholars who adopted feminist approaches to understanding gender and sexuality (Allison 1994; Bellér-Hann 1995; Hart 1997; Kulick 1998; Manderson 1992; Scott 1995).

Feminist anthropology, with its keen attention to the cultural constructions of gender and sexuality, presented a sharply focused lens through which these anthropologists could observe the complex intersections between gender, socioeconomic power, and desire as experienced by diverse individuals. Quite a bit of this earlier scholarship also engaged with the then-nascent sex workers' rights movements (Brock 1998; Gal 2006) as well as with then-current debates surrounding sexuality. Subsequent sex work research built upon these earlier works to examine the nuanced meanings of transactional sex for those who engage in it. There are many outstanding sex work researchers who have engaged in ethnographic research in various branches of social science and public health, but in the interests of brevity the ensuing discussion will situate anthropologists' book length ethnographies into broad thematic categories, focusing predominantly upon the chief contributions each has made to the discipline.

Some of the most vividly written and compelling scholarly publications on sex work follow anthropologist Lila Abu-Lughod's encouragement to construct ethnographies of the particular. Abu-Lughod drew upon feminist critiques of objectivity and power by Donna Haraway and Dorothy Smith in conceptualizing the "ethnography of the particular", which conspicuously avoids a focus on the theoretical and analytical in favor of recreating the complex nature of everyday life. In doing so, Abu-Lughod sought to "(a) reveal something important about the relationship between what is often called structure and agency, and (b) disclose the incapacity of structural analyses" (2000, p. 262).

Ethnographies of the particular have proven especially powerful in studies of sex work because of their capacity to illuminate both the specificities of place and accompanying normative moral frameworks, as well as the nuanced lives of participants in the research. Through this heavily descriptive form of ethnographic writing, anthropologists are able to depict the aspirations and occasionally counterproductive decision-making processes that sociologist Avery Gordon refers to as "complex personhood" (1997), which acknowledges that "even those who live in the most dire circumstances possess a complex and often contradictory humanity and subjectivity that is never adequately glimpsed by viewing them as victims or, on the other hand, as superhuman agents" (1997, p. 4).

In her work on a state-regulated brothel in Chiapas, Mexico, employs this style of ethnographic writing to position her interle human beings struggling to negotiate the neoliberal forces that restrict their lives through increased state surveillance while simultaneously offering seductive promises of the ability to consumption-related practices. Zheng (2009) also utilizes the ethnography of the particular in describing the lives of rural migrant sex workers in Dalian, China, thereby situating these women as aspiring to urbanity just as they serve as a way for men to demonstrate status and prestige in a new market economy. Writing of sex workers and their clients in a Spanish city,

Hart (1997) explores how both of these populations make sense of their "deviant" status in uniquely gendered ways.

Medical anthropologists have also tackled the question of gendered identity construction among sex workers, often by situating some form of sex work as part of a broader nexus of homelessness, addiction, and other forms of exclusion. Yasmina Katsulis demonstrates how public health regulations on prostitution in Tijuana work to differentially disenfranchise and stigmatize sex workers by their citizenship status and social class. Much ethnography that focuses specifically upon the public health aspects of sex work is in article form, and often explores street or survival sex work.

Medical anthropologists Bourgois et al. (2004), for instance, have explored the intersections between drug use, gendered vulnerabilities, and sex work in San Francisco. Orchard (2012) focuses upon a similar population in her research on motivations for beginning sex work and subsequent experiences of marginalization and violence in a mid-size Canadian city. In a rare African context, Izugbara (2010) documents Nairobi sex workers' notions of good health as well as their strategies for reducing risk through client retention.

Anthropologists, like feminist theorists in other disciplines, have also considered sex work as a form of feminized labor due to the reality that sex workers are primarily female and labor in a service industry that caters to men. In this line of thinking, Frank (2002) investigated the meaning that male clients ascribe to exotic dance through both her research and her own work as a nude dancer. Day (2007) documented London sex workers' ways of thinking about sexuality both in and outside of the money economy, thus building upon enduring feminist debates about distinctions between public and private life. Building upon this work, I carried out fieldwork at a topless bar in the economically devastated Rust Belt region of New York State as a site of feminized labor that was just one piece of how dancers negotiated motherhood and relationships (Dewey 2011).

A more limited body of research explores sex work that is performed by men or transgendered persons. Kulick (1998) pioneered this area of inquiry in his work on gender performance and stigma among Brazil's *travesti*, biological males who transform their bodies through silicone injections and other dangerous procedures that they pay for through funds generated by engaging in sex work. While *travesti* self-identify as female and desire physical intimacy with heterosexual men, this is not the case for all sex workers. Frembgen (2008), for instance, has described how heterosexual-identified Muslim masseurs in Punjab perform a culturally stigmatized role, not unlike the *travesti*, by providing a space for their straight-identified clients to experience homosociality and sexual pleasure.

The anthropological literature on male sex work can also be situated within a broader genre that examines sex work within a broader array of international socioeconomic relationships, particularly tourism. Allen (2011), for instance, describes the lives of Afro-Cuban men who trade sex for money with affluent male tourists and wealthier urban Cubans as part of a self-making project that combines both desires for commodities and upward social mobility. Based upon research in the Dominican Republic, Padilla (2007) examines the work of young men who eke out a living in "the pleasure industry" of a tourism-based economy that also involves sex work. Mitchell (2012) investigates similar questions in Brazil, where his work on straight-identified men who have sex for money with gay and bisexual tourists as a means to support families and participate in a consumer economy.

Conceptualizing tourism as a form of migration that may lead to other, more permanent forms of migration, Brennan (2001) writes of Dominican sex workers' hopes for social mobility through sex with foreign men. Cabezas (2009) similarly describes what she terms a "comingling of sex, intimacy and market forces" in Cuba and the Dominican Republic. Through its keen attention to everyday lives of individuals who engage in behaviors that either resemble or actually constitute sex work, such work directly problematizes discourse that frames such migration as "trafficking", a term that positions such migrants as little more than victims devoid of agency in a wide variety of geographical and cultural contexts (Day and Ward 2004; Zheng 2010). Pardis Mahdavi (2011) builds upon this work in her juxta-position of sex workers' and other labor migrants' accounts of their experiences in Dubai with anti-trafficking rhetoric of governments and international organizations, finding sharp disconnects between the two. I have similarly examined these disjunctures between intention and effect in my work on international organizations' responses to sex trafficking (Dewey 2008).

A related body of literature emerged from anthropologists who have explored these disconnects in the form of local moralities and their impacts upon sex work-related public or state policy. Hanna (2012), for instance, unpacked the ways in which religious and political discourses shape local concerns regarding the supposedly deleterious impacts that strip clubs have upon surrounding neighborhoods. Her analysis highlights how moral opprobrium, rather than evidence, can have a profound impact upon sex work's legal status. This topic has been explored further in an edited volume that interrogates cross-cultural public policies related to sex work and the disjunctures that occur between intention and effect (Dewey and Kelly 2011).

Montgomery (2002) also pursued this line of critical inquiry in Thailand, where she worked with Thai children who engaged in sex with tourists to support their families. International responses to this issue, Montgomery argues, emphasized the horror of child sexual abuse in ways that did not reflect the experiences of children and their families, many of whom lived in poverty so abject that sex work was the most palatable work option available to them. Montgomery contends that the broader discourse that emerged from Western Europe and North America regarding childhood sexual slavery ignored the deeper socioeconomic conditions that facilitate child sexual exploitation. The fact that the abuse involved sex, it seemed, was much more interesting to media and activists than the other, perhaps even more painful, aspects of the children's lives.

While all of the ethnographic texts mentioned here pay attention to the ways in which sex work is embedded in local cultural histories and norms, some focus particularly keenly upon this issue. Nencel (2001) does just this in her discussion of the "gendered enclosures" that shape sexuality and sex work in Peru through particular types of discourse and physical sites that function to perpetuate stigma in particular ways. Building upon this discussion of local histories and cultural norms, Wardlow (2004) situates Huli "passenger women" in Papua New Guinea as agents who actively resist sexist social structures that render them as *olsem market* (market goods) to their husbands and biological families. Wardlow argues that some Huli women engage in sex work as a means of achieving some measure of autonomy from family members who otherwise control their sexuality. However, Wardlow notes, such women keenly experience stigma and marginalization in ways that severely limit their abilities to participate as full members of Huli society.

The preceding literature review underscores that anthropological research on sex work has become increasingly diverse and sophisticated in recent years. As participants in a burgeoning field that probes evermore nuanced and difficult issues, sex work researchers find themselves constantly negotiating ethical issues that defy conventional solutions.

Ethical Challenges in Sex Work Research

The on-going debates between sex workers' rights advocates, who often employ a harm reduction approach or view sex work as a form of legitimate labor, and abolitionist activists, who generally understand sex work as a form of violence against women, make our consideration of ethical issues in sex work research particularly timely (Valverde 1987; Weitzer 2010). Anthropologists who study sex work are firmly positioned in the midst of these debates as they endeavor to conduct research that prioritizes the worldviews and cultural knowledge of research participants. Hence a researcher working with, for instance, undocumented migrants who engage in sex work as an income generation strategy faces a serious set of ethical questions. How, for example, should the researcher present her (or his) findings in ways that prioritize the migrants' experiences as the migrants themselves understand them? Does the researcher have a responsibility to contest claims that such migrants are "victims of trafficking" by presenting her (or his) evidence-based research in particular publication venues? And, perhaps most importantly, could the researcher's presence potentially threaten the migrants' well being by drawing attention to their living conditions and income generation strategies?

Many researchers have found that it is now a political act to present the words of sex workers who view their labor as the best choice open to them, as doing so could potentially open their work up to virulent criticism by abolitionists. On more than one occasion, social scientists have been accused of serving as apologists for behavior that abolitionists gloss as "trafficking" by engaging in research with sex workers and presenting their findings on sex workers' terms. This criticism has taken the form of very public denunciations of such work at professional conferences, on listservs, and in scholarly journals.

Social scientists, including anthropologists, have been accused of serving as apologists for behavior that abolitionists gloss as "trafficking" by engaging in research with sex workers and presenting their findings on sex workers' terms.

This has taken the form of very public denunciations of such work in scholarly journals, at professional conferences, as well as on listservs and organizational websites. While these stories tend to circulate informally among sex work researchers rather than being published, these abolitionist-led attacks can have professional repercussions, particularly for younger scholars who have not yet received tenure or, due to an increasingly constricted academic job market, a tenure-track position.

Sociologist Ronald Weitzer's work constitutes perhaps the best and more thorough critique of the use of anecdotal or otherwise biased research methodologies by abolitionists. Some abolitionist research has resulted in law and public policy that reflects an understanding of sex work as a form of violence against women (Weitzer 2010). Weitzer describes the body of research produced by such academics and activists as one in which the "canons of scientific inquiry are suspended and research deliberately skewed to serve a particular political agenda. Much of this work has been done by writers who regard the sex industry as a despicable institution and who are active in campaigns to abolish it" (Weitzer 2005, p. 934).

In a response to this critique, psychologist Melissa Farley, an abolitionist activist, called Weitzer "a supporter of indoor prostitution" (2005, p. 952). The following extended passage from one of Farley's publications exemplifies the abolitionist view of sex work as inherently violent, no matter where it takes place:

> What is wrong with prostitution cannot be fixed by moving it indoors. The same harms are there whether she is in a trick's house, a back alley, his car, or a room at a hotel. And the same physical violence occurs whether it is in a pimp's massage parlor, the private booth of a pimp's strip club, a pimp's legal brothel, or a pimp's street turf. The same psychological violence occurs indoors, too- none of that changes based upon the location of the prostitution. She still gets called vicious names while he is masturbating in her, those names that as one woman said, "cut you like a knife", so that she has to get high or she must dissociate to tune out the poison. Weitzer's apologetics for and evasions of this reality cannot obscure it (Farley 2005, p. 964).

Farley's descriptions of sex workers' plight as victims of abuse so severe that their only recourse is retreat into substance abuse or mental illness places the blame squarely upon a group of individuals she terms "pimps", a word she does not define. In the work of Farley and her abolitionist colleagues, sex workers are abused, pathetic and, above all, incapable of making their own choices and hence in dire need of protection. Sex workers' rights activist and academic Jo Doezema describes this discourse as one in which "the paradigmatic image is that of a young and naïve innocent lured or deceived by evil traffickers into a life of sordid horror from which escape is nearly impossible" (Doezema 2000, p. 24). Such claims gain substantiation through research design and methodologies that focus upon sex workers' violence and victimization, which reflects itself in study findings that, in turn, impact law and public policy.

Women's Studies academic and activist Donna Hughes, whose work has received funding from prestigious sources including the National Science Foundation and the Department of Justice, exemplifies the abolitionist approach. Like many other self-identified abolitionists, she argues that envisioning prostitution as a choice involves a form of false consciousness, in which an individual or group experiences severe marginalization that results in an inability to see their experiences as oppression:

> Prostitution and trafficking are extreme forms of gender discrimination and exist as a result of the powerlessness of women as a class. Sexual exploitation is more than an act; it is a systematic way to abuse and control women that socializes and coerces women and girls until they comply, take ownership of their own subordinate status, and say, "I choose this". Prostitution and trafficking restrict women's freedom and citizenship rights. If women are treated as commodities, they are consigned to second-class citizenship. No state can be a true democracy if half its citizens can potentially be treated as commodities (Hughes 2000).

In Hughes' assessment, the existence of sex work, particularly prostitution, poses a danger to the rights of all women and reflects a social system that privileges men.

Research designed upon the premise that sex work-related behavior is inherently violent and damaging will likely result in findings that corroborate this philosophical perspective. Sex workers' rights activist Norma Jean Almodovar asks what would happen if all knowledge about marriage was based upon research undertaken with married women living in domestic violence shelters (Almodovar, personal communication). Such women would likely have a very different perspective on marriage than happily married women, and some abused women might even argue that marriage is a flawed institution that puts women at great risk for physical harm.

Almodovar notes that if a researcher felt deeply invested in abolishing marriage, she (or he) might even intentionally exclude from the study women who had not experienced violence in their marriages. Focusing solely upon survivors of intimate partner abuse might indeed yield substantial evidence that marriage causes harm to women: indeed, the Centers for Disease Control and Prevention's National Intimate Partner and Sexual Violence Survey indicates that there are over 12 million incident of intimate partner violence and one million intimate partner rapes each year (CDC 2010).

Almodovar chooses marriage, a practice that many, if not most, adults engage in at some point in their lives, as an example precisely because such a study would be so ridiculous due to intrinsic flaws and lack of a representative sample. Yet such biases persist in research by abolitionist scholars. Concerns about the ethics involved in such research practices prompted Queer Studies scholar and organizer of the New Zealand Prostitutes Collective Calum Bennachie to file a formal complaint against Melissa Farley with the American Psychological Association, the organization that oversees her home discipline. In it, he alleged that she did not seek ethical or other research approval from any of the countries in which she conducted her research, that she consistently misstates or uses inaccurate statistics, and that a highly structured questionnaire employed in her research focused exclusively upon violence and harm (Bennachie 2010).

Abolitionist scholars have responded to these allegations of research bias by denouncing any criticism as anti-feminist and pro-sex work; on occasion, these denunciations have included personal attacks, threats of lawsuits, or outright refusal to engage in dialogue with others who do not share their opinions. ıch responses have taken place in extremely public forums, including scholarly journals, academic conferences, and in postings on organizational websi have resulted in an environment which many sex work researchers feel that they have become the targets of a very vocal group that enjoys considerable institutional and financial support.

Sociologist Gail Dines and her colleagues responded to a negative review of two recent books on pornography (one of which was written by Dines) with the rather thinly veiled accusation that the reviewer, Ronald Weitzer, was a sexist. In his review, Weitzer criticized the books' lack of transparent methodological approaches to the subject matter and dismissed the authors' findings as based in ideological assumptions rather than empirical researcher. Dines' response noted that reading Weitzer's review "catapulted me back to my undergraduate days when the ideas of credentialed White men were considered objective scholarship, while the rest of us were dismissed as producing ideology-laden arguments based on anecdotes" (Dines 2012, p. 512). Philosopher Lori Watson, in a second rebuttal to Weitzer, characterized Weitzer's call for more empirical research on pornography as "the lowest form of academic criticism: Aim to discredit your opponent by asserting that her work simply is not "scholarly" work, but the view of an unlearned, unsophisticated, and perhaps hysterical woman" (Watson 2012, p. 505).

Such heated exchanges have also taken place following calls for evidence-based legislation and public policy. One particularly disturbing example followed a petition to the Rhode Island State Legislature regarding a bill that would make all indoor prostitution illegal in the state. The petition, signed by fifty academics (including one of this book's co-authors), stated that research clearly demonstrates that sex workers were safer and healthier when working in legal indoor environments (Henry 2009). A response written by a group called Citizens Against Trafficking, headed by Donna Hughes, dismissed the petition's authors in a statement on the group's website, which called them "sex radicals...targeting Rhode Island for their own extreme sexual libertarian agenda of preventing any legal limits on any sexual behavior" (Brooks and Hughes 2003, p. 3). Just as Dines and Watson dismissed as sexist a negative review of ideologically based research, Hughes impugned the moral character of the petition's signatories, many of whom were middle-aged tenured professors who spend the vast majority of their waking hours working and would hardly self-identify with the term "sex radical", or who might chafe at the idea that they endorse a policy of "preventing any legal limits on any sexual behavior".

Other researchers, activists, and scholars have experienced more extreme threats, including litigation, as did research scientist and former escort Brooke Magnanti as she awaited the publication of *The Sex Myth*, her first book written under her real name (Magnanti 2012). Magnanti published the previous four books under the pseudonym "Belle de Jour", the name she used while writing a popular blog which chronicled her life and work as a London escort (Belle de Jour 2006, 2008, 2009, 2010). She envisioned her new book as an evidence-based refutation of some of the most common myths surrounding sexuality as well as an examination of the ideological impact that such beliefs had upon law and public policy. As part of the work she carried out for the book, Magnanti examined detailed government reports regarding funds allocated to anti-trafficking groups, and argued that these amounts far exceeded the scope of the problem in the United Kingdom.

The day before book's scheduled publication date, Magnanti's publisher received an email from an abolitionist group accusing her of libel. The accusation quoted at length from the book and pointed out an error Magnanti had made in one of her statistics related to the group; while this error did not affect her conclusions, the group claimed that its inclusion constituted an intentional attempt to reduce their credibility. Magnanti's publisher opted to delay the book's publication by two weeks in order to correct the error, during which time she faced additional accusations from the group that she had illegally obtained their records (when in fact she had relied upon material posted publically on their website). The publisher eventually decided to proceed with publication following the determination that these legal threats were nuisances designed to halt the publication of the book. However, the threat of litigation remains a serious concern for researchers working in this area, and places serious limits on academic freedom to present empirical research findings that contradict the assumption that large number of women and girls are forced into sex work against their will.

A sex work researcher who wishes to remain anonymous characterized her conference experiences with anti-pornography activists as "bullying", involving a level of confrontation and anger far exceeding the norms at professional academic events. The researcher and her colleagues feel that they have been attacked and derided, both in print and in person, for pointing out flaws in the research designs used in various anti-pornography studies. She further notes that:

> The attacks are often well coordinated and, at times, quite vicious, creating a climate where it takes nerves of steel to do what in most academic circles is simply considered part of the job: discussing the strengths, limitations, merits, and shortcomings of any given piece of research. To do so in the context of sexuality research requires knowing in advance that you are stepping into a potential minefield where you - rather than just your ideas or research - might be subject to attack.

Media scholar Alan McKee echoed some of these concerns regarding abolitionist responses to his Australian Research Council-funded work on pornography (Lumby et al. 2008). McKee's work relied upon surveys and interviews with pornography users and content analysis of this media genre, positioning those familiar with the subject matter as authorities of their own experiences with it, which is standard practice in social science research. Feminist human rights scholar Helen Pringle objected this use of standardized methodologies to study pornography on the following grounds:

> The research project elevated the opinions held by pornography users to the status of "expertise", and characterized their practices as the acquisition of valuable knowledge. This required in turn the construction of pornographic materials as "harmless"- after all, we do not consult racists in formulating laws against hate speech on the basis that they are involved in and know a lot about racism (Pringle 2011).

The less-than-subtle connections Pringle draws between pornography users and racists links both as equally morally repugnant characters unworthy of academic investigation.

Anthropological principles of cultural relativism make it less likely that ethnographic researchers would face attack by those from within their home discipline for engaging in sex work research. However, abolitionist critiques in other venues, such as interdisciplinary conferences, still pose a threat to sex work researchers' academic freedom. One anthropologist experienced this form of silencing at a national conference following her presentation, in which she argued that many participants in her research described sex work as the best out of a series of other limited life options. During the question and answer period, an audience member pointed angrily at the anthropologist and shouted, "It's because of people like you that women are raped and imprisoned as victims of trafficking", before storming out of the room.

This is not an isolated occurrence. At an undergraduate-organized conference held in 2010 on current issues in human trafficking held at a small liberal arts college, students invited several noted scholars, activists, and policy-makers for a series of debates, discussions, and lectures. These included anthropologists Thaddeus Blanchette, Tiantian Zheng, Gregory Mitchell, and prominent sex workers' rights activist Carol Leigh, who were all critical of various aspects of anti-trafficking discourse. Representatives from anti-trafficking NGOs, including Polaris Project, Doctors at War, and Global Centurion, were also present as well other groups focused on related forms of trafficking such as Invisible Children, which later became famous for its Kony 2012 campaign.

While most of the organizations' representatives engaged in civil (if sometimes spirited) disagreement about sex trafficking, one leading scholar and featured speaker referred to the movie *Lilja 4-Ever* (Moodyson 2002) as a true story and described its content as factual evidence. Blanchette and Leigh were filming the conference events, and when Blanchette challenged the speaker's claim, noting that the film is a fictionalized account, she became angry and demanded that filming stop. The undergraduates spoke with the conference presenters a few hours later, quite distressed, and reported that this featured speaker left the conference, threatening to sue them and to write to the college administration in an effort to have the students punished, blaming them for the public embarrassment she felt she suffered. Although, in the end, the college stood firmly behind its students and no actions were ever taken, this threat was intended to have a cooling effect and to discourage students from including dissenting views at future events, as well as send a message to Blanchette, Mitchell, Zheng, and Leigh that if they challenged prominent anti-trafficking advocates, they might bring harm to host institutions, students, untenured colleagues, or themselves.

An article in *The Chronicle of Higher Education* described significant differences in research findings in two studies of Nevada's legal brothels, the first by sociologists based at the University of Nevada Las Vegas (Brents et al. 2009), and the second by psychologist and founder of the abolitionist Prostitution Research & Education founder Melissa Farley (2007). As the reporter noted,

> One key difference between Ms. Farley's research and that of the UNLV scholars lies in how they approached the responses offered by the prostitutes they interviewed. When women had positive things to say about their work, the university researchers generally

took such responses at face value, while Ms. Farley often dismissed such answers as the product of dissociation- a mental tuning out of negative feelings as a coping mechanism-based not on any formal psychiatric diagnoses but on other researchers' work on victims of trauma (Schmidt 2011).

Farley dismissed the UNLV researchers' findings as a consequence of their "working with pimps" in interviews with brothel owners and managers, and for interviewing sex workers inside brothels, where "they might have had reason to fear surveillance and repercussions for speaking candidly about their jobs" (Schmidt 2011). During a visit to Las Vegas to promote her book, which she self-published through the abolitionist organization which she founded, Farley met with numerous media outlets that subsequently publicized her claims of exploita-tion in Nevada's legal brothels, all without consulting the UNLV researchers who spent nearly a decade formulating the research findings presented in their peer-reviewed book and numerous academic journal articles (Goldman 2008).

Such a hostile environment has the potential to make researchers cautious of how they present their findings, and how and with whom they undertake collab-orative work. These, in and of themselves, constitute powerful ethical dilemmas that researchers must seriously consider before they even begin formulating their research questions. Researchers must ask themselves if they are willing to risk libelous accusations of sexism, immorality, or threats of lawsuits when their find-ings do not corroborate the abolitionist assumption that all forms of sex work con-stitute violence against women.

Many social and behavioral scientists would agree that ethical research com-prises a carefully designed set of methods, procedures, and perspectives that directly inform research-related decision making, conduct, and analysis, including norms for conduct that distinguish between acceptable and unacceptable behavior (National Institute of Environmental Health Sciences 2011). Yet anthropologists know all too well that such notions of acceptable and unacceptable vary enor-mously from group to group. As one of the participants in my street sex work pro-ject succinctly summarized this issue with respect to her time in the prison system following a conviction for drug possession, "Everything that's right inside [prison] is wrong outside."

Yet just as anthropology's core principle of cultural relativism empowers researchers to express sex workers' own views without engaging in solipsism, this notion of relativity can also complicate ways of thinking about ethics. Anthropologists' strong adherence to cultural relativism, in fact, can make it diffi-cult, or even counterproductive, to judge the behavior of others in the field, or to clearly understand when one's own behavior has potentially crossed ethical lines. I know that, for instance, crack cocaine use is a relatively normal part of street-based sex work in one of the cities in which I am currently carrying out fieldwork; I also know that the street-based sex workers I speak with deserve some form of compen-sation for time they spend speaking with me. I struggle with having the authority to determine the most appropriate form of compensation, feeling guilty because I hesi-tate to provide cash (however small the amount) rather than a meal because cash can much more readily be used to purchase crack. I ask myself whether my decision is condescending, as if I somehow know, from my position of relative privilege, that a meal is a better use of ten dollars than is a small rock of crack.

Because anthropologists deal in the business of human life, often with stigmatized or criminalized populations, ethical lines are rarely fixed. Anthropological research with sex workers can be fraught with ethical difficulties throughout all stages of the research process, from the initial project design to the dissemination of results. While anthropology is a discipline that places a high value on the cultural specificities of place, researchers must be cognizant of the way that others might make use of their research results once published. Hence it is critical that sex work researchers attempt to develop well-balanced research samples that adequately represent the diversity of labor and cultural practices described as sex work. This is particularly significant given that sex workers may alternate between or simultaneously combine one or more forms of sex work that present significantly different levels of risk (Reuben et al. 2011; Wesley 2003).

The resulting ethical dilemma for researchers entails the risk of having their results, which have been garnered from one specific sex worker population, speak to the experiences of all sex worker populations with the potential for negative public policy and legal outcomes. The academic literature in public health, criminal justice, and the social sciences, for instance, emphasizes that street-based sex workers frequently experience higher rates of violence (Campbell 2001; Church et al. 2001; Dalla et al. 2003; Day and Ward 2001; El Bassel et al. 2001) and significantly increased chances of homicide-related death (Potterat et al. 2004; Brody et al. 2005; Quinet 2011; Salfati 2009; Salfati et al. 2008; Brewer et al. 2006) than others who do not engage in this form of sex work.

The reality that such extensive academic research has been carried out with street-based and survival sex workers means that much of this knowledge has the potential to be generalized to larger sex working populations. This is significant because strippers, escorts, peep show performers, and other sex workers employed in venues that provide them with greater discretion and security generally do not report violence as their main concern, although stigma and discrimination remain factors that can diminish their quality of life (Bradley 2007; Brents et al. 2009; Egan 2006; Sweet and Tewksbury 2000).

Yet part of the reason that street-based sex workers have been studied so extensively is that they are more readily accessibly due to the ease with which researchers can locate such individuals in jail, homeless shelters, addiction treatment facilities, or in urban neighborhoods that function as informal prostitution tolerance zones (Inciardi and Surratt 2000; Miller 1993; Romero-Daza 2003; Surratt et al. 2004). The already murky ethical territory of sex work research is exacerbated by the reality that street-based sex work often takes place in low income, minority, or otherwise disadvantaged neighbourhoods with a history of negative interactions with dominant institutions. Additionally, there is also the potential for research to further stigmatize and sustain social prejudices against historically oppressed groups, including sex workers themselves (Chapkis 1996). It could be argued that researchers have an ethical responsibility to avoid perpetuating sex work-related stigma in their research design, methodology, and dissemination of findings.

Yet researchers should be wary of labeling sex workers a "vulnerable population", as sex workers of all kinds clearly participate in social networks that may alternately support and abuse them, including biological or fictive kin (Dalla 2001, 2003; McClelland and Newell 2008; Sloss and Harper 2004) and individuals who self-identify as "pimps" (Norton-Hawk 2004; William and Cluse-Tolar 2002). Researchers have likewise documented sex workers' strategies for negotiating risk and danger (Roche et al. 2005; Sanders 2004; Williamson and Folaran 2003).

It can be difficult for relatively privileged academic researchers to establish trust with individuals who have had a consistent experience of marginalization by those in positions of power (Pettiway 1996, 1997), which, in turn, places a strong moral and ethical imperative upon researchers to endeavor to develop inclusive research methodologies, a topic which is discussed in depth in Chap. 4. Even when this trust is established through long periods of researcher embeddedness in the field, U.S. mandatory reporting laws, such as those concerning child abuse and neglect, can raise serious ethical concerns for researchers who find themselves witnessing or hearing about such behavior in the course of their research (Dunlap et al. 2009). Such laws require researchers to report suspected cases of minors involved in sex work to law enforcement.

Researchers also have the ethical responsibility to minimize the risks of interpersonal and structural risks that participating in the research might incur. While not all countries have Institutional Review Boards (IRB) that approve or deny research proposals based upon the potential risks and benefits posed to participants, all North American and many Western European sex work researchers must consider these risks and ethical issues in a formal IRB application well before they begin their research. Potential risks to the research participants that may concern an IRB run the gamut from emotional consequences such as re-traumatization or psychological distress, to risk of arrest for participants. While researchers sometimes regard the IRB as an impediment to innovative research or as not fully understanding of issues involved in ethnographic work with stigmatized populations, this process cannot be avoided and thus might be more positively regarded as an opportunity to fully consider all of the risks that the proposed research might entail.

Consideration of the potential risks that the research could pose to participants comprises an essential component of both ethical research design and IRB proposals at most academic institutions. Emotional distress caused by interviews that could potentially delve into sensitive territory is a very real ethical concern. While not all sex workers have had experiences with violence, the vast majority of sex workers are cognizant that they perform a highly stigmatized form of labor that others may judge as immoral or criminal. This stigma has a powerful impact upon some sex workers notions of their own social interactions and sense of personhood.

This recognition involves a form of structural violence that can cause emotional distress in its own right. During the course of an interview with a former survival sex worker in New Orleans, even my use of phrases or terms like "sex worker" or "prostitution" proved a point of contention that caused me to quickly reconsider whether I could ever hope to speak to individuals with such different perspectives

structural violence
of stigma

with a single interview protocol. After my second mention of the term "prostitution", she looked directly into my eyes and said slowly, "Those are some big
words you throwin' down- if you talkin' about the sex thing, that's just one way
some women get by out there." Hence participating in research may have emotional consequences, whether in the form of feeling compelled to recount behaviors that cause shame or embarrassment, or very real trauma-related consequences.

I witnessed this first hand while living in shelter with a group of women who
had chosen to leave sex work either because they were aging out or due to addiction problems they felt ready to address. One day when I dropped a glass on the
kitchen floor and uttered a less-than-polite expression of my disappointment at the
mess I had made, shelter resident and former street sex worker Kayla's shoulders
visibly tensed and she shook her head sharply at me. "Girl," she said, "it really
takes me back when you talk like that. That kind of language is a trigger for me."
Another woman concurred with Kayla, saying that what they called "street talk"
did not belong in shelter, which they felt was both a physical and a discursive space
separate from the norms and language of their former world of street sex work.

Kayla's use of the word "trigger", although a common term in the more therapeutic realms of social services, evokes violence in its rather deliberate analogous
use of the part of a gun that propels a bullet on its deadly path. Shelter residents
used the word to describe behaviors, speech patterns, or visual cues that prompted
them to vividly re-experience trauma they had previously experienced. These trig-
gers included particular body postures and facial expressions as well, particularly
what some women called "crack mouth", which involved widening the lips in a
fish-like motion that some recovering addicts in the house associated with smoking crack cocaine.

The ethical dilemma presented in this instance is quite nuanced: in my use
of profanity I violated norms that I failed to fully grasp, and yet I had also made
Kayla and her roommate feel victimized at some level. Interviews with individuals
who a researcher does not know well present myriad other possibilities for similar
difficulties. While I had the luxury of getting to know Kayla and others at shelter,
our relationships would have been very different had I interviewed them in a motel
room or at a bus stop, two locations that they had formerly frequented as street-
based sex workers. Risks, not unlike emotions, are very personal and individual in
nature, and what constitutes sensitive subject matter to one person might be fodder
for casual conversation for another.

Kayla, for instance, often criticized other shelter residents for telling "war stories", the phrase she used to describe tales related to sex work and drug use that
she felt glorified or made light of the trauma that the individuals experienced in
these situations. Conversely, her friend Kristi enjoyed spending evenings smoking
cigarettes with me on the porch and laughing as she recounted the rollercoaster of
emotions and events that accompanied a typical night in her crack use and street-
based sex work career. Unlike Kayla, Kristi envisioned herself as a tough survivor
and found great strength in telling these stories, which I think she felt emphasized
her ingenuity and almost uncanny ability to charm others into giving her what she
wanted.

Researchers bear an ethical responsibility to consider these enormous variations in the ways that individuals understand and emotionally process their experiences of sex work. When reviewing my interview protocol with a local representative of the Sex Workers Outreach Project (SWOP) prior to starting research in a new city, the SWOP representative recommended that all questions avoid asking the interviewee anything about her direct experiences. Hence instead of asking a respondent to discuss her own experiences with the police, I asked, "What kinds of experiences have some of the people you know had with the police?"

This slight change in the wording of the question, as the SWOP representative explained to me, allowed each respondent to choose how much she wanted to reveal about her own experience with sex work. Such a strategy protected women like Kayla, who saw sex work as a traumatic and painful period in her life, as it allowed her to speak about other women she knew while working in ways of her choice, that did not force her to disclose anything about herself. Women like Kristi, however, chose to answer all the questions by citing their own experiences, often going on at length about problem solving and survival skills she had learned along the way.

Collaborating with a sex workers' rights organization before beginning the project enriched my thinking about the unique dynamics of sex work in a new city tremendously by encouraging me to move beyond my previous research experiences and consider new perspectives. The preliminary work I engaged in while designing the project involved meeting with dozens of social service providers who encountered sex workers in the course of their professional duties, which informed me about services available in the city and also provided me with an opportunity to identify sex worker-friendly services in the city to which I could refer women I met during my research who felt that they needed some therapeutic or mental health counselling. I included contact information for such service providers on my informed consent form, which sex workers did not have to sign in order to completely protect their identities, and were free to keep at the end of our interview.

While I negotiated the powerful impact of stigma on sex workers' lives by engaging in a great deal of preliminary research prior to beginning the project, this advance preparation made me realize the potential difficulties in obtaining accurate self-reported data on sexual and other health-related practices. I learned much about the risks to street-based sex workers' health and safety from my preliminary meetings with health and social service providers, but street-based sex workers did not describe the same set of risks in my conversations with them. In fact, to hear the street-based sex workers tell it, the only public health risk posed came from *other* street-based sex workers who were so deeply embedded in their addictions that they cared little about condom use. Street-based sex workers I spoke with almost never implicated themselves as individuals who occasionally did not use condoms.

This highlights an ethical dilemma for sex work researchers, who may find themselves torn between their desires to collect data on, for example, condom use among street-based sex workers, and their knowledge that their research participants may over-report condom use. While most sex workers believe that condom use significantly reduces risks to their health, their ability or willingness to practice safer sex depends upon access to condoms, ability to negotiate condom use, and cultural (as well as interpersonal) understandings of condom non-use as an expression of trust and intimacy (Vanwesenbeeck et al. 1994). Additionally, police officers in some U.S. cities refer to condoms as "prostitution paraphernalia" and use condoms possession as evidence of involvement in sex work, further impeding sex workers' abilities to protect themselves as part of a pattern that has been globally replicated via USAID stipulations that US-funded organizations explicitly "oppose prostitution", sometimes through foregoing condom distribution (Chang 2011).

Researchers thus confront an ethical dilemma of using self-reported information on sexual behavior, even when they are aware that research participants may not always accurately report their own behaviors due to the high levels of stigma they face. They may fear judgment or, more simply, they might simply have no desire to disclose highly personal information to a relative stranger. As sex work researcher and activist Laura María Agustín puts it:

> ...keeping secrets may help sex workers gain independence or control over projects to help them. Talking about sexual risks with people who think it's wrong to ever take *any* risks may cause them to treat you as irresponsible. Admitting the desire to stay in sex work after getting out of the clutches of abusers can render you ineligible for victim- protection programs. The best policy may be to omit certain information from responses or to put on the expected front (Agustín 2004, p. 6).

A secondary and related dilemma for those researchers who work with drug users or addicts involves their compromised ability to provide accurate information or wish to participate in research due to the criminalized and stigmatized nature of their activities. Research demonstrates that some, but by no means all, sex workers engage in drug abuse, and that addiction strongly correlates with street-based sex work in many urban locales (Shannon et al. 2007; Edwards 2006; Golder and Logan 2007; Sherman et al. 2011; Spittal et al. 2011). This presents a significant ethical dilemma in terms of remuneration for research participants who may use the funds to engage in self-harming behaviors such as substance abuse as well as in terms of producing meaningful results when research participants may engage in the study for the sole purpose of obtaining money to buy controlled substances.

Sex work research participants who struggle with substance abuse or addiction may have very different perspectives on risks and benefits than those in positions of relative privilege who design and carry out research on the subject (Porter and Bonilla 2009). Yet researchers may confront additional ethical dilemmas with such populations when the question of the duty to inform arises for researchers who may observe the sharing of needles between those whose HIV status they know and those they do not (Fisher et al. 2009; Buchanan 2009). In such populations, homelessness or precarious housing often correlates with substance abuse (Caputo 2008; Duff et al. 2011; Erickson et al. 2000; Maher and Curtis 1992).

Indeed, the realities inherent in low community cohesion among sex workers presents a unique set of challenges regarding research, particularly in environments where sex worker colleagues may not know each other's legal names or whereabouts. This high degree of mobility can impact sex workers' interactions with researchers, resulting in an ethical dilemma regarding how best to maintain contact with research participants while simultaneously acknowledging their desire to remain part of a relatively clandestine population. Researchers must struggle with the question of how to determine whether their participants want to be contacted again should they cease communications with the researcher who, after all, is likely a low priority on most research participants' lists of immediate concerns.

A more serious ethical concern involves the potential risk of a researcher inadvertently causing harm in a sex worker's interpersonal relationships. This could happen through a researcher's bringing attention to an individual's sex worker status without realizing that not everyone in her (or his) life may be aware of these activities. Researchers should implement a set of universal precautions in their work may help to alleviate this risk somewhat by assuming that most sex workers only selectively disclose their income generating activities.

The researcher should always wait for instructions from a sex worker regarding where, when, and to whom it is appropriate to disclose particular information that she (or he) has shared with the researcher. Having these conversations can serve as a rapport-builder and could also prove instructive for a researcher as she (or he) attempts to understand the complexities involved in sex workers' lives. Similarly, researchers must recognize and act to minimize the potential for disrupting street-based sex workers' income generating activities in their attempts to build rapport. For these sex workers, the street is their workplace and it should be treated as such.

Respecting sex workers' privacy is an ethical responsibility that researchers should take very seriously. This is especially true of researchers who expect to become deeply involved in sex workers' everyday lives, where they run the risk of unintentionally causing interpersonal discord in attempts to establish rapport. Researchers must be mindful of the risks that their presence presents to sex workers, some of whom work in conditions where it may not be safe to talk to well-meaning anthropologists. For instance, there is usually no way to definitively tell from observations alone if a sex worker is involved in a violent or otherwise coercive relationship, researchers should remain attuned to this possibility in order to avoid causing further harm.

There are some precautions that researchers can take in order to minimize the risk of causing harm to sex workers who may not feel free to speak to researchers for a number of reasons, including control by a pimp. In a relatively public sex work venue, researchers should never approach a sex worker who displays avoidance behavior, such as stepping away, averting her eyes, or otherwise employing body language that demonstrates a desire to be left alone. A researcher can never know the reasons for her behavior, and in such a situation it is advisable to avoid causing any unintended harm by approaching her.

While this overview has served to briefly introduce some of the ethical challenges anthropologists may face in their research with sex workers, subsequent chapters will explore these issues in depth. There are clearly no right or easy answers to many of these ethical dilemmas and, as the rest of this book will clearly demonstrate, researchers may frequently find themselves relying upon their own individual moral compass as they navigate the ethically fraught terrain of sex work research.

Chapter Overview and Structure of the Book

This book aims to provide a thorough overview of ethical issues anthropologists may face in sex work research. Chapter 2 engages with the ethics surrounding research questions, confidentiality, informed consent, methodologies, representative research samples, and data reliability. This chapter discusses issues faced by sex work researchers in the initial stages of research project planning, particularly in the formation of research questions and methodologies that actively seek to reduce the gap between researcher and participants. It proposes research design strategies for accessing representative sex worker samples and explores the utility of engaging in smaller scale ethnographic studies with particular sex worker populations.

Chapter 3 discusses the difficulties researchers face in carrying out work in a politically and ideologically charged environment in which they must remain constantly attuned to the legal and public policy implications of their work. The passage of U.S. federal anti-trafficking legislation and its numerous international counterparts in the past decade has created a legislative and public policy environment that frequently conflates all forms of sex work with trafficking, broadly defined as the use of force, fraud, or coercion to induce one's participation in sexual labor.

These legislative developments and concomitant political debates directly impact sex work researchers, who find themselves confronting danger and stigma while at the forefront of extremely contentious debates between self-identified abolitionists, who view sex work as a form of violence against women, and sex workers' rights activists, who contend that sex work is both an enduring reality and an individual choice deserving of the same amount of respect accorded to any form of labor. This chapter also explores ethical practices related to reciprocity and reflexivity.

Chapter 4, co-authored with the New Orleans and Las Vegas branches of the Sex Workers' Outreach Project (SWOP), envisions possibilities for participatory sex work research processes by drawing upon both SWOP's extensive expertise in working with sex workers and previous scholarly work employing related approaches. In the politically charged environment that surrounds sex work, it is no surprise that some researchers are keen to engage in work that actively incorporates the perspectives of sex workers on equal terms with that of the researcher. This chapter will describe such researchers' strategies for incorporating participants in a variety of collaborative ways, from research design to the dissemination of findings, identifying challenges and strengths in each approach.

As demonstrated in this introductory overview of ethical issues that may potentially arise through anthropological engagement with sex work, such research presents a unique set of challenges that are not always well understood by those working outside of anthropology and disciplines closely related to it. We hope that this book will serve an important function by honestly and openly reviewing strategies for overcoming these ethical challenges with the end goal of producing path-breaking research that actively incorporates the perspectives of research participants on their own terms.

Actively involving research participants in this way is likely to result in more nuanced research results that are more likely to produce recommendations for policy change. We have boundless respect for our colleagues who engage in sex work research, and consider this book a collaborative effort resulting from many years of conversations on ethics with our colleagues and participants in our own research. Ever attuned to the reality that research on sex work remains a deeply political act, the ensuing chapters aspire to begin a dialogue about the meanings and practices ascribed to ethics in a fraught environment.

Chapter 2
Ethical Research Design

Tiantian Zheng

As Punch noted (1994, p. 84), ethnographic research is "potentially volatile, even hazardous, requiring careful consideration and preparation before someone should be allowed to enter the field." This is especially true in research with marginalized, stigmatized, and often criminalized groups of sex workers on deeply private, sensitive, and sexual issues and behaviors. In which case, researchers are faced with a plethora of moral and ethical dilemmas, such as confidentiality concerns, informed consent, and representative samples.

Due to a dearth of resources that can guide sex work researchers through this process, this chapter fills the lacunae and provides a detailed analysis of key ethical concerns during research design. More specifically, this chapter explores issues faced by sex work researchers in the initial stages of research project planning, particularly in the formation of research questions and methodologies that actively seek to reduce the gap between researcher and research subject and ensure that the researcher will not exploit or harm research subjects. It discusses research design strategies for accessing representative samples of sex workers and the utility of engaging in smaller scale ethnographic studies on particular sex worker populations.

The very nature of the phrase "sex work" in itself presents an ethical dilemma for researchers, as this umbrella term rarely conveys the diversity of behaviors, beliefs, and activities, both legal and illegal, that it encompasses, and consequently presents a risk of the experiences of one particular group of sex workers being generalized to others who have a very different set of norms, behaviors, and beliefs. Ethical research design also necessitates that researchers minimize risks to both participants and themselves. This chapter accordingly assesses ways in which sex work researchers endeavor to do this, while also drawing upon my ethnographic research with sex workers in China. Below I will discuss the ethics of formation of research questions, confidentiality, informed consent, research methodologies, representative research samples, and reliability of data during the insipient research planning stage.

S. Dewey and T. Zheng, *Ethical Research with Sex Workers*,   23
SpringerBriefs in Anthropology and Ethics,
DOI: 10.1007/978-1-4614-6492-1_2, © The Author(s) 2013

The Ethics of Research Questions

The "feminist sex wars" that depict sex workers as either victims or liberated women have influenced the kinds of research questions many sex work researchers explore and the way they frame the questions theoretically. Many researchers investigate similar research questions about power and exploitation such as "Do sex workers or clients have power?" or, "How is power exercised or negotiated?" In answering these research questions, some researchers perpetuate the two extremes of exploitation and liberation, while others challenge the dichotomy and argue that power relations are complicated and sex workers occupy a space on a continuum between the two extremes.[1]

While power is often the central area of research inquiry for sex work researchers, many sex work researchers delve into a list of subsidiary research questions. Jacqueline Lewis (2000, p. 204) states that the literature on deviant behavior usually investigates three analytical areas of inquiry: factors for entry into deviance, ways to cope with stigma, and negotiations between customers and workers. Indeed, in probing the answer to the central questions about power, many sex work researchers pose the following subordinate research questions: Why do women engage in sex work? What factors influence their decision? What kinds of stigma are associated with the occupation? How do sex workers manage the stigma? What are the patterns of interactions between sex workers and clients? What is the impact of sex work on sex workers' lives? How is the working condition in sex work? Indeed, the vast literature on sex work has explored these questions in different sectors of sex work. For instance, in the sector of strip dance, researchers have studied entry factors, working conditions, stigma management, and ramification of the work on sex workers' lives (Frank 2002; Barton 2006; Deshotels and Forsythe 2006; Wesely 2003; Thompson et al. 2003).

In view of the ubiquitous central research question of power, I recommend that sex work researchers, in formulating their own research questions, confront their own preconceived ideas and eschew making absolute, moral judgments about exploitation and agency. This calls for a more complex and nuanced conceptualization of power and agency. Instead of posing the research question of who has the ultimate power, I encourage researchers to explore questions such as how

---

[1] Consider the case of Ming, a woman I came to know through my research in China. After working in a club as a hostess for 5 years, she received a marriage proposal from one of her clients who was the CEO of a five-star hotel chain in China. She accepted his offer and ceased all work in the sex industry upon marriage. After taking up residence in a very affluent Beijing neighborhood, Ming became pregnant and had a child. Shortly afterward, she resumed her hostess work behind her husband's back. Eventually, a great fight broke out when the husband became aware of his wife clandestine activities. The conflict was resolved only after she promised that she would never again engage in sex work. When I asked Ming why she chose to jeopardize her financial security by working as a hostess, she said it was because she loved the attention she received from her clients. This example vividly illustrates how the simplistic view of sex workers as oppressed victims is untenable.

and when sex workers negotiate power and agency with customers, what kind of power and agency sex workers enjoy vis-à-vis customers, and how customers and sex workers can mutually empower and exploit each other (see Sloan et al. 1998; Lewis 2006; Frank 2002).

In addition to avoiding research questions that over-simplify and over-generalize sex workers, I recommend that researchers go beyond questions about power and agency to explore other areas of inquiry. These might include multiple dimensions of the sex workers' subject positions, clients' motivations and perspectives, marriage between clients and sex workers, wives of male clients, boyfriends of female sex workers, and social and cultural change concomitant with sex work such as reconfigured meanings of romance and intimacy (see also Frank 2007; Zheng 2009). These inquiries have rarely been explored and warrant detailed analysis in order to understand how sex workers are embedded in multiple layers of social, cultural, political, and economic contexts.[2]

For instance, in my own research on sex workers in China, I have investigated and theorized these areas of inquiry. On the topic of cultural change, I have examined the women's value changes after their engagement in sex work, and the complex tension between sex workers' commoditized romance and their longing for a "true" romance. On the topic of clients, I have delved into clients' motivations and clients' wives' perspectives, and illustrated the intricate relationships between sex workers, clients, clients' wives, and the state (Zheng 2009). I have shown how clients select their business alliance members through watching their consumption of women's services and assessing their qualities. I have demonstrated how the relationships between clients and their wives mirror the relationships between clients and the state.

Likewise, I have also depicted the women not only as sex workers, but also as multilayered and multipositioned subjects who are rural women in the countryside, migrant women in the city, dominant sisters in the family, and filial daughters for the parents (Zheng 2009). Indeed, I have demonstrated that it is impossible to understand the women's behaviors, life styles, and occupation without exploring their complex subject positions. More specifically, it is the political restraints and cultural stigma attached to the status of rural, migrant women that have led these women to appropriate sex work to refashion a modern and industrial identity, carve out a legitimate space in the city for themselves, and debunk the stereotype of them as country bumpkins without cultural tastes (Zheng 2009).

There are many more new realms of inquiry that are worthy of research. The goal is to delineate an ethical, multifaceted, and multilayered picture of sex workers' lives lived in specific contexts, and bring to afore their hopes, fears, struggles, successes, and failures.

---

[2] Frank (2007, p. 511) notes that there is little research that addresses how strip club visits are integrated with customers' workplaces and workplace practices, ethics, or environments, and how the wives or partners of male regular customers make meaning of the men's visits. Zheng's research on sex workers (2009) has dealt with both issues ethnographically in the entertainment industry.

Confidentiality

In his writing about the use of life stories to study deviance, Lee (1993) notes that such research poses potential harm and threats to research subjects, which may inhibit or enhance data collection. Lee (1993) discusses the fears of research subjects that researchers may disclose information to authorities, and that these authorities may impose sanctions on their behavior or punish them in other ways.[3] Indeed, research of sex workers is fraught with such ethical and methodological challenges. The stigmatized, marginalized, and often criminalized nature of the research subjects renders the issues of confidentiality and privacy especially more crucial than other areas of study (see also Shaver 2005). It is researchers' responsibility to ensure research subjects' confidentiality and privacy.

Confidentiality refers to the protection of the anonymity of research subjects during research and during public dissemination of research results. To ensure confidentiality, it is crucial for researchers to create a mechanism during research design to protect and disguise research subjects' identities. Precautionary measures can include but are not limited to: using pseudonyms for individuals' names and places, utilizing large sample sizes, and transferring data to a secure email account. It is also critical not to use videotapes or cameras on research subjects or research sites that may compromise subjects' identities. In certain situations where both the researcher and the participants feel it is appropriate, taped interviews may be conducted upon receiving participants' informed consent. Researchers could then collaborate with participants in reviewing and editing interview transcripts to increase the quality of the data. At the same time, the process can empower participants and enhance mutual trust between researchers and participants (see also Cwikel and Hoban 2005).[4]

Protecting confidentiality is the cornerstone of a trusting relationship between researchers and participants. Participants may not release honest or reliable information if they do not trust researchers' ability to protect the information from the authorities. Therefore, to achieve research goals, it is indispensible that researchers cultivate a trusting relationship with research subjects. The mutual trust fostered and built in the long-term fieldwork will not only ensure researchers' intense

---

[3] Lee (1993, p. 4–11) identifies three broad areas of risks to research subjects. First, research may pose an intrusive threat (1993, p. 4) due to nature of the research topic as private, secretive, and stressful. Second, the study of crime or areas of social control can incriminate or marginalize research subjects upon disclosure of the information. Third, 'political' matters can involve political interests of people and organizations.

[4] Cwikel and Hoban (2005) state that in their research with trafficked women working in the sex industry, instead of using electronic recording of interviews, they use two people to conduct interviews. One person conducts the interview and the other records information. In situations where they are able to tape interviews with informed consent, they provide the women with transcripts of the interviews for feedback and editing right after the interview. As Cwikel and Hoban (2005) contend, this practice helps improve the reliability of the data and assure confidentiality of interviewees.

participation and observation in participants' working and private lives, but also allow participants to divulge secretive, sensitive, and personal information to researchers. It is researchers' responsibilities to follow ethical guidelines and keep confidential the acquired information and participants' identities.

Data such as direct quotes of participants' words and detailed life stories of participants in publications should also be handled in a delicate fashion so that the use of raw data would not unwittingly disclose their identities (see also Corbin and Morse 2003; Creswell 2008; Damianakis and Woodford 2012; Etherington 2007; Kaiser 2009; Tolich 2010). It is potentially possible that people who are familiar with the participants could identify certain information, such as detailed life story narratives, and hence compromise or even give away participants' identities.[5] Such risks of breach of confidentiality should be explained to participants at the beginning of the research.

It is essential that researchers are aware of the power in published research results to potentially harm participants and communities. Researchers should not only keep the anonymity of the people involved in the research, but also represent their voices in a fair and accurate way to maintain confidentiality and integrity of the research. It is important that researchers are cognizant of potential risks that the government, media, or organizations could appropriate or misuse the data against sex workers.

Some researchers such as Hearn and his colleagues argue that confidentiality cannot and should not be absolutely maintained for legal and moral concerns (Hearn 1998; Hearn et al. 1993). They denote three approaches to confidentiality: legal, moral, and research. They contend that on legal and moral grounds, researchers, if they fail to report criminal activities such as rape, violence, and child abuse, could be charged with aiding and abetting criminals and interfering with the law (Hearn 1998; Hearn et al. 1993).

Informed by such concerns, researchers such as Cowburn (2005) address this dilemma by emphasizing to the participants at the outset of his research that the information would be confidential unless the participants have admitted an offence they have had committed and have not been prosecuted for, or the participants have indicated a risk to themselves. Cowburn (2005) makes it clear to the participants that he would report them to the Prison Service in both cases. He believes that the legal and moral obligations are sufficient grounds for researchers' breach of confidentiality of research subjects.

I disagree with such a position and believe that researchers should exert all efforts to maintain absolute confidentiality and minimize any harm or risk the research could potentially inflict on research subjects. Due to the sensitive topic

---

[5] Arlene Stein (2010) discusses the dilemma about keeping the confidentiality of her research subjects and research community, and the consequence of the breach of the confidentiality of the research community as a result of the publication of her book. Stein (2010) believes that if she had not promised anonymity to her research subjects, she would have been able to avoid the controversy arisen from the breach of the confidentiality.

and stigmatized participants, the collection process, storage, and public dissemination of the research data could potentially pose threats or risks to research participants (see Lee and Renzetti 1990). More specifically, divulged research information could help identify, incriminate, and further stigmatize those studied. In view of the risks to research subjects, I argue that all social scientists should abide by the fundamental principle of cultural relativism and maintain their role as objective observers. They should strive to lessen the effect their study has on the people and studied culture through nonintervention and noninterference.

Sex workers, like any other vulnerable and stigmatized populations, are fearful of the legal consequence of imprisonment and cultural consequence of ostracism upon the exposure of their identities. During my research with sex workers and clients, I learned about rape occurrences and illegal activities, witnessed physical violence inflicted upon sex workers, and found myself hiding with the women in illegal brothels during police raids. The perpetrators of rape, physical violence, and illegal acts were bouncers, clients, ex-convicts, managers, and government officials. Corrupt law enforcement officials often took advantage of sex workers' fear of incarceration and coerced sex workers to comply with sexual services.

During the course of my fieldwork, sex workers were often subject to physical abuse by bouncers, clients, and managers. Witnessing the women being physically beaten yet not being able to intervene made me feel powerless and heartbroken. Indeed, many of my informants had visible injuries from physical abuse on their bodies. Due to the criminal law against sex work, reporting to the police would be tantamount to disclosing the identities of the sex workers, which would subject them to imprisonment, stigma, rehabilitation, loss of survival means, and severe fines. Acutely aware of the potential harm my violation of confidentiality could inflict on my informants, I chose to be a vulnerable observer (Behar 1997)[6] and maintained full confidentiality of all my participants without any limitations.

At the outset of my research, I assured the sex workers, establishment owners and managers that I was a researcher and would keep their identities and interview materials in strict confidence. I also made it clear that the published findings would fully protect their individual anonymity as well as the anonymity of all others involved in the research. To make sure that my research did not place the business or the people at risk, I used pseudonyms for names and places. Indeed, the sex workers used false names anyway, which I called "operating pseudonyms". Some women told me their real names but I never requested or recorded their real names.

Additionally, I kept the key linking pseudonyms to participants' operating pseudonyms in a safety box hidden in my apartment. I kept the key separate from my records, which I transferred to an email account registered under another name several times a week. I also destroyed any remaining hardcopies of my records. Gaining access to my data would therefore necessitate that someone to break into my apartment, destroy a safety box, discover my email pseudonym, and gain

---

[6] Behar (1997) champions the notion of the anthropologist as the "vulnerable observer", who is compelled to work through his or her emotional involvement with research subjects. .

access to that email account in order to compromise the confidentiality of my participants' identities, a highly unlikely series of events. Given the large sample size I worked from, access to the records would make it practically infeasible for an outside party to piece together the identity of my informants. Because my precautions reduced the risk of exposure to a negligible level, participants to the study were effectively anonymous.

Since researchers rely on the consent of brothel owners and managers to conduct research, it limits researchers' ability to intervene on the business and the lives of the people involved. Researchers can only record research data and minimize the effect their presence has on the business. Any intervention may result in incarceration, deportation, and stigma of the sex workers, physical danger for the researchers, and termination of the research at the brothel.

Informed Consent

Informed consent is a critical procedure to ensure participants' rights and confidentiality and to protect them from undue harm associated with the research (Miller and Wertheimer 2007). In the procedure, researchers are required to provide participants with full information about the research, and allow participants to question the researcher and exercise autonomy in participating in the research, rather than coercing or deceiving them into it (Bhutta 2004). More specifically, prior to the research, researchers must explain to the participants the purpose, process, and methods of the study, the use of the data, the potential costs and benefits the study has on the participants, the protection of confidentiality not to do any harm, the protection of participants' rights to voluntarily participate in the study and withdraw at any time. Upon receipt of participants' informed consent, researchers can begin their research. Standard procedures advise that researchers write up a statement about the research and have participants sign the written, official form, indicating their consent to participate.

Informed consent is especially paramount when the research topic of sex work and the marginalized sex worker community involve risks for participants. In my own research in China, I chose to orally present informed consent in the informants' language. I introduced my identity as a researcher, the nature, length, and methods of my research, participants' rights, and potential costs and benefits of the research to the sex workers, clients, establishment owners, and managers. Some suspected that I was a spy from the U.S. or a journalist. I assured them that I was not any of those and I explained in detail the ways in which I would keep their identities and the research data confidential.

I also informed them that despite my efforts to safeguard confidentiality, it was still possible that a third party, the police, or other forms of state authorities might be able to link their identities with narratives of their life stories and interviews. I warned them that if this were to happen, any information regarding illicit activities that they had provided me might place them at risk for legal sanctions and possibly incarceration. I also explained to them that participation was completely voluntary and that they could choose at any time to discontinue their participation in this study. I then asked if they had further questions about this informed consent and whether they agreed to participate in the study.

I chose verbal consent instead of written consent forms. There were two reasons that I did not ask the participants to sign any consent forms. First, the informants were not willing to sign their names on the consent forms, as it would put their identities as risk. Second, the sex workers operated under pseudonyms because of their illegal work and illegal rural migrant status. During research design, I was cognizant of their double illegal status. As rural migrants, they were required by law to purchase the temporary resident card from the city government. Many of them evaded the fees and kept an illegal residency in the city. They could potentially be discovered by police through random inspections on the street or through raids on the establishments to check for the temporary resident card. Noncompliers with residency rules always ran the risk of being caught, deported, or imprisoned. My goal was that my presence and my research would neither increase this risk nor impede law enforcement officers from performing their duties.

Since I had already obtained the informed consent from the establishment owner and managers, I did not need to pursue further consent from visitors to the establishment. The establishment was a public place, and visitors were mobile and transient. Further consent from these visitors was no longer necessary as the owner and managers had consented to my research and my participation in the establishment. I was allowed to record my observations and evaluations of public behaviors in the public setting of the establishment.

However, it would be wrong to assume that informed consent is a once-and-for-all activity prior to the research. Rather, informed consent represents a dynamic, ever-changing process throughout the research. As the relationship between researchers and participants deepen, the boundary of the informed consent needs to be reevaluated and redefined. Informal settings and informal dialogues could potentially subject participants to the risk of unwitting disclosure. Therefore, it was important that researchers and participants were both aware of the boundary between public and private discourse (see also Seal, Bloom and Somlai 2000). In some cases, researchers showed participants the final product of the research and obtained the informed consent prior to the public dissemination of the research.

During my research, informal conversations provided me with a great deal of information. It was my responsibility to identify the nature of the information provided. If the information was a general statement and did not involve secretive, context-specific, personal information, I would not procure informed consent. However, throughout my research, some informants saw me as a confidante and released a great deal of personal, secretive information that could potentially compromise their confidentiality. In these situations, it was my duty to seek and acquire further informed consent to incorporate the data in my research.

To uphold ethical principles while producing rigorous research, ethical researchers need to be vigilant of the nature of the information provided and recognize potential violation of confidentiality upon its publication (see Stein 2010).

Ethics of Research Methodologies

Researchers' preconceived ideologies can lead to methodological flaws and result in over-simplified and generalized arguments about sex workers. Indeed, embracing either of the dichotomized positions of exploitation or liberation can circumvent researchers' ability to explore and collect data. To avoid engaging in warped methodologies, I recommend that researchers not only respect the validity of sex workers' statements and experiences, but also evade alliance or collaboration with organizations and institutions that hold certain political views about sex work. The political bias of the organization or institution could potentially distort the research methodologies and research design.

Methodologies informed by the dichotomized theory tend to perpetuate the polarized view of sex workers as pure victim or pure agents. The ideological differences can skew the kinds of interview questions, research focus, and research result (van der Meulen 2011). Indeed, if the researcher views sex workers as victims of oppression, research methods tend to situate sex work in a moral context and center on how to end the sex industry. Interview questions would be designed to focus on unfair work practices, problematic labor conditions, and violent working environment. The data collected in this manner would focus on violence and ignore the diversity of experiences of sex workers (Parsons 2005; Wahab and Sloan 2004). In the end, the distorted research findings would reproduce the degrading and victimizing view of sex workers and argue that the entire sex industry is exploitative and should be abolished as a whole, an outcome that may not reflect the beliefs and experiences of the research participants (van der Meulen 2011).

Due to the bias inherent in such research methodologies, some researchers continue to pathologize, demonize, and criminalize sex workers' experiences and behaviors (Farley 2007). They portray sex workers as victims in need of protection and rescue and unable to make decisions about their lives and work. Their research instills suspicion, distrust, and frustration in sex workers and divides sex workers and sex work researchers.

To overcome the methodological bias and dismantle the barrier between researchers and sex workers, researchers need to eschew moralistic judgments and respect sex workers as both experts on their lives and active agents who are capable of making informed decisions as well as making changes in their lives. Researchers should include sex workers' experiences and seek their advice on how to ameliorate their working conditions and improve political policies. Such a methodology can help bridge the gap between sex workers and researchers and enhance sex workers' collaboration with researchers (Wahab 2003).

Sex work researcher Wahab (2003) points out three reasons for applying such a methodology to treat sex workers as experts. First, researchers have repeatedly denied the validity of sex workers' statements. Second, experiences of stigmatization and marginalization can potentially imbue sex workers with the wisdom to understand their lives. Third, it is indispensible that feminist research places women and their lived experience at the center of inquiry (Wahab 2003, p. 630). In short, to ensure that research methodologies are not tempered or overshadowed by ideology, researchers need to employ an inclusive approach that can involve sex workers in the analysis and interpretation of their lives, behaviors, and life choices.

Representative Research Samples and Data

One of the methodological challenges for sex work researchers involves acquiring representative research samples due to the fact that the size and demographic compositions of sex worker populations largely remains unknown and diverse (Shaver 2005). Shaver argues that this problem cannot be solved by the traditional methods of sampling of sex workers: snowball sampling, key informant sampling, and targeted sampling. The first method of snowball sampling, she maintains, can produce biased results since it only draws more cooperative participants who may have ulterior motives for participation. In the second method of key information sampling, she asserts that information generated from social service agencies, health care workers, and police also reflects stories of sex workers who are in trouble.

As a result, sex workers who are less interested in the research and who are not in trouble are rarely reported. The third method of targeted sampling is used when the researcher successfully infiltrates the sex workers' population in the local network. In this method, Shaver states that there is a possibility that the most visible sex workers such as street workers are over-reported and the less visible ones who work inside are under-reported (Shaver 2005).

To address the issue of representative research samples of sex workers and ensure the authenticity of data, I make the following recommendations. First, sex work researchers need to be aware that the sex industry is diverse and broad. Second, if possible, it is important that sex work researchers gain access to the sex workers in their most representative setting and in their natural environment, with a critical analysis of the limits and biases of the sample. Third, to enhance the reliability of the data, I recommend that sex work researchers corroborate stories told by sex workers with information provided by their partners, family members, clients, and establishment managers and workers.

It is possible that sex workers and other relevant informants, pressured by the stigmatized behaviors and concerns about privacy and confidentiality, may choose to lie or tell researchers what they think researchers would like to hear. To minimize such challenge to the validity of data, it is imperative that researchers confirm the data with the informants' family, friends, partners, and local network. The multiple data sources allow researchers to increase the validity and reliability of the data (see also Cwikel and Hoban 2005).

In my own research, to obtain representative samples and reliable data, I lived and worked with bar hostesses as a hostess myself in an underground brothel of a karaoke bar for an entire year (Zheng 2009). I shared with the women the same risks and obstacles of police raids, arrests, rape, and violence. I shared with the women the same frustrations and miseries from waiting on customers. I relied on the women's advice and expertise on how to thwart customers' sexual advances and how to refuse customers' request for sexual services. Escaping arrests and police raids together and sharing tears and laughter from the job experience pulled us together as friends rather than as researchers and subjects. I visited many women's rural hometowns, stayed in their families for a long period of time, and befriended their boyfriends, clients, and friends. Talking to their family members and local network friends turned out to be extremely helpful for me to verify the women's accounts, discern and analyze the discrepancies, and identify and correct the false information provided to me.

For instance, one of the hostesses had the right half of her face scarred and paralyzed. She told every other hostess in the bar as well as her boyfriend and me that her ex-boyfriend had slashed the right half of her face because she had wanted to break up with him. As a victim of male violence, she earned empathy from us and we frequently offered her money since she was not often chosen by clients.

One night when we had dinner together with a couple of hostesses, she became drunk and confessed to us that she was born with the scarred face. We were confused, but later on she said she was talking nonsense because of the influence of alcohol.

Faced with the two disjointed stories, I visited her hometown and stayed there for half a month. During that time, her mother told me that she was twenty six, not twenty-one as she had told everyone in the bar, and that she was born with the scarred face. It turned out that her biological mother had an affair with a married man and had become pregnant with her. She had taken abortion medications, which were taken too late and failed. Her biological mother gave birth to her in a bathroom and abandoned her. Her current mother took her away from the bathroom and adopted her. She said the scars did not show up on her face until she was four or five years old. The scars were the consequences of the attempted abortion.

In another story, while a client bragged to me about how his hostess lover was devoted to him simply because of his charm ever though he did not bestow gifts or money on her, she later showed me all the merchandises he had bought her, including costly necklaces, cutting-edge mobile phones, and money.

These two stories showed the importance of validating and corroborating research subjects' stories with people in their family and social network.

I chose to sample the karaoke bar hostesses from their natural working environment, but did not lose sight of the diversity of the industry and the unique characteristics of the sector. Indeed, a wide array of erotic services take place in various establishments that include karaoke bars, hotels, saunas, hair salons, disco and other dance halls, small roadside restaurants, parks, movie houses, and video rooms. Diversities not only exist across these sectors, but also within one sector (Zheng 2009, p. 79–104). Within one sector such as karaoke bars, there is a class hierarchy that is defined by the management and organization, the locale, the clientele, the spending level, the level of violence, and the number, beauty,

educational level, and turnover rate of hostesses. Across sectors, the sector of karaoke bars demands the most stringent criteria for the women's height, facial beauty,
figure, and such social skills as singing, dancing, flirting, drinking, and conversation. Unlike what is provided by the other sectors where only sexual intercourse is
offered, karaoke bar hostesses' services are far more encompassing.

Only a few of the karaoke bar hostesses would accept strangers' request for sexual intercourse, for which they charge twice as much as is charged in many other
environments except for a few five-star hotels targeted at Japanese clients. Because
only the beautiful and skilled can be chosen as company for the night, numerous
young women could not survive in karaoke bars and are thus forced to move to less
desirable workplaces and skidded to other places such as sauna salons. Fully aware
of their own status second only to foreign hostesses such as French and Russian
in renowned hotels, karaoke bar hostesses often express contempt toward women
working in other sectors whose work involves nothing but sex.

As discussed, to develop a nonexploitative and nonbiased method during the
research design phase, researchers should be aware of the diverse nature of the sex
industry and refrain from generalizing one sector of sex work to the entire industry. Weitzer (2000, p. 4) cautions that, "when it comes to prostitution, the most
serious blunder is that of equating all prostitution with street prostitution, ignoring
entirely the indoor side of the market". Researchers should keep this caution in
mind during research design.

To eschew the erroneous notion that sex workers represent a homogeneous
population, researchers are advised to design comparisons or other methodological approaches to reflect the heterogeneous nature of sex work. Indeed, similar to
my work, other works have also recorded not only the diversity between sectors of
the sex industry, but also the diversity within each sector (Benoit and Millar 2001;
Browne and Minichiello 1996; Whittaker and Hart 1996; Chapkis 1997; Nadon
et al. 1998; Perkins and Lovejoy 1996; Shaver 2002, 2005). As Shaver contends
(2005, p. 299),

> …comparisons are essential if we are to fully understand the challenges they face and the
> social, political, and economic processes creating and maintaining those challenges. They
> will help identify which of these challenges are unique to sex work (and sex workers)
> and which are features of more general conditions, such as gender, ethnicity, educational
> opportunities, health status, and poverty.

Research on sex work has informed us that social and cultural factors such
as class, gender, management control, and location affect the nature of sex work
and sex workers' experiences. For instance, Hoang's ethnography of sex work
in Vietnam delineates three racially and economically diverse sectors of the sex
industry in Ho Chi Minh City (2011). The three sectors include a low-class sector
catering to poor local Vietnamese men, a middle-tier sector catering to white back-
packers, and a high-end sector catering to overseas Vietnamese men. Hoang argues
that the nature of sex work differs in the three sectors. While sex work in the low-
class sector involves economic exchanges, sex work in the middle and high tiers
involve romantic and intimate exchanges that have developed through continuous
interactions between sex workers and clients.

Sex workers' profile, agency, and experiences also vary in the three sectors (Hoang 2011). In the low-class sector, it is the poor rural and urban women who engage in sex work to escape poverty. They are paid little for sexual exchanges and often find the work unappealing. In the middle-tier sector, sex workers posses more economic resources than those of the low-tier sector. They engage in both sex-for-money exchanges and cultural exchanges with white clients from the U.S., Europe, and Australia. Sex workers, who have English skills, often engage in relational exchanges with clients such as serving as their tour guide and cultural broker. They purposefully develop the relationships into romantic relationships to get married to their clients and migrate abroad.

According to Hoang, in the high-end sector, sex workers are from relatively wealthy families. Most have a university degree. Some receive financial support from parents, and many have high paid salary jobs in the city. These women are able to freely exercise their power in deciding whether and under what conditions they will have sex with their clients, and whether and under what conditions they will continue the relationships with their clients. They often withhold sex, and when they do engage in sex, they project themselves as girlfriends of the clients and conceal their status as sex workers. They meet and spend time with clients in high-end consumption sites, where they are already able to afford drinks and services. Their goal is to continue enjoying a wealthy lifestyle sustained by their clients.

As illustrated, class is certainly one of the many factors that reveal variegated meanings of sex work and heterogeneous experiences of sex workers who share different backgrounds, different experiences, and different abilities to exercise agency and power. Research has shown that other elements such as gender, location, management control, and the type of sex work also exert an impact on these differences. To name a few, Shaver's comparative research of three gendered groups of sex workers of females, males, and transgendered persons exhibits gender differences and undermines perceptions of homogeneity (2002).

Research by Shaver and Weinberg (2002) also explores regional differences due to policy differences, tolerance differences, and varied access to sex workers' rights groups. Numerous researchers also report that sex workers working on the streets or outdoors (including call girls) experience less workplace freedom and more physical violence, competition, police arrests, and health risks than sex workers working indoors, including brothel workers (Chapkis 2000; Whittaker and Hart 1996; Jackson et al. 1992; Pyett and Waif 1997; Perkins and Lovejoy 1996).

Other comparative studies also indicate that management control and the type of sex work can negatively or positively impact the working environment. For instance, sex workers working independently exercise more power than sex workers working in agencies in determining labor costs, net earnings, clients, working hours, and sexual activities (Benoit and Millar 2001). In another example, sex workers working in the peep show, due to the glass barrier between sex workers and their clients, enjoy more power and control over their performance than sex workers working in strip clubs who are under constant surveillance by the management (Chapkis 2000).

When facing the challenges presented by the myriad diversities that character-ize the sex industry, researchers need to identify appropriate groups for compari-son, access the most representative sample in their natural working environment, and augment the trustworthiness of data through corroborating the data received from sex workers with sex workers' family networks and clients.

Conclusion

Since sex work researchers will encounter many ethical challenges during research, a detailed analysis of these ethical issues during the insipient stage of research design is beneficial in designing nonexploitative research with sex work-ers. Indeed, research design with a special heed to ethical concerns can provide researchers with a certain degree of expertise in dealing with ethical issues and moral dilemmas arising from fieldwork. Due to the stigmatized and marginalized nature of sex work, researchers are faced with ethical challenges such as the for-mation of research questions, confidentiality, informed consent, minimized risks and harm, diversity of the sex industry, research methodologies, representative sample, and reliability of the data. As illustrated in the chapter, researchers can resolve these challenges with a variety of strategies that have been proven effica-cious in sex work research such as my own.

In formulating ethical research questions, researchers should evade research questions that over-simplify and over-generalize sex workers. I have recommended that researchers go beyond the questions about power and agency and charter new areas of inquiries. I have used my own research and other sex work research to identify the under-explored, yet worthy and significant realms of inquiries such as the complex subject positions of sex workers, clients' motivations, clients' wives' perspectives, the diversity of sex workers' experiences, and the diversity of the sectors of the sex industry. A scrutiny of these complicated dimensions of sex work can help tell a multifaceted, multilayered story of lives engulfed in specific social, political, and economic contexts.

The goal of an ethical research project is to protect participants from harm while respecting their human dignity (see also Shaver 2005). During research design, researchers are advised to adopt risk-reduction guidelines such as confi-dentiality and informed consent to protect the anonymity of participants. In this chapter, I have explored some ethical issues related to confidentiality and informed consent. Although researchers can be witnesses to violence and illegal acts, I rec-ommend nonintervention to minimize the risks for participants and guarantee full confidentiality without any conditions or limitations.

It is essential for researchers to obtain participants' autonomous, informed con-sent before carrying out the research. Researchers also need the informed consent from the establishment owner and manager in order to record their observations of the setting as research data. Informed consent from all participants involved in the research is by no means a one-time procedure, but an ongoing process, especially after the researcher–participant relationship develops and the boundary between public and private knowledge becomes blurred. Researchers need to be vigilant of the secretive and sensitive contents that participants reveal to them and seek further informed consent from the participants to include these contents in the research data.

In order to overcome the methodological bias and bridge the gap between researchers and sex workers, researchers need to jettison their preconceived values that could potentially distort research methodologies and collect misrepresented research data. To avoid methodological flaws spawned by researchers' preconceptions, I recommend that researchers treat sex workers as experts and active agents who can make informed decisions and make changes to their lives. If possible, researchers should also eschew collaboration with organizations and institutions that hold certain political views about sex work and research design.

To ensure the quality of data, researchers need to increase the representativeness of the sample, adopt a comparative strategy, work in sex workers' natural working environment, penetrate their local, family, and client networks to verify the data, and immerse themselves in participants' everyday lives. A strategic comparative study across sectors or within a specific sector is also crucial to undermine the stereotype of sex workers as a homogeneous population by delineating the complexity and diversity of the sex work industry and the sex worker population.

A further ethical methodology to reduce the gap between sex workers and researchers is to include sex workers in the research design, research process, data collection, and final stage of data dissemination. This will be fully addressed and discussed in Chap. 4. Whether a researcher chooses to engage in participatory research or not, she (or he) should be mindful of ethical considerations at all stages of the research design process. Doing otherwise runs the risk of further marginalizing and reinforcing stereotypes about sex workers, who already face considerable stigmatization and social discrimination.

Chapter 3
Ethical Research in a Fraught Environment

Tiantian Zheng

No matter what type of sex work researchers study and the depth of their efforts to protect their research participants, sex work researchers operate in a politically and ideologically charged environment in which they must remain constantly attuned to the legal and public policy implications of their work. The passage of U.S. federal anti-trafficking legislation as well as its numerous international counterparts in the past decade has created a legislative and public policy environment that frequently conflates all forms of sex work with trafficking, broadly defined as the use of force, fraud, or coercion to induce one's participation in sexual labor.[1]

This directly impacts sex work researchers, who find themselves at the forefront of extremely contentious debates between self-identified abolitionists, who view sex work as a form of violence against women, and sex workers' rights activists, who contend that sex work is both an enduring reality and an individual choice. In this chapter, I will first discuss the kind of ideologically and politically charged environment sex work researchers work in. I will then explore the impact of such an environment on sex work researchers' abilities to obtain Institutional Review Board approval, access the sex industry, and maintain safety in the field. I will follow the analysis with a recommendation of the ethical strategies of reciprocity and reflexivity for researchers to cope with the ideologically and politically charged research environment.

An Ideologically Charged Environment

Sex work researchers are faced with contemporary debates that have been ongoing for at least three decades without any sign of a resolution in sight. These polarized positions frequently portray sex work as either good or bad, and sex workers

---

[1] For more information on the critique of the dominant anti-trafficking discourse with ethnographic accounts of women's lived experience around the globe, please see Zheng (2010).

liberated and empowered workers or exploited, coerced victims Sloan and Wahab 2000; Meulen 2011; Vanwesenbeeck 2001). This vision of sex workers originated from the 1980s feminist "sex wars" nationally and internationally, with dramatic and sometimes detrimental impacts upon law and public policy.

Abolitionist discourse on sex work is heavily informed by the work of feminist theorists such as Catherine MacKinnon (1987) and Andrea Dworkin (1987), who argue that men's abuse of their own male privilege is inherent in any transactional sexual exchanges, a belief system that recognizes prostitutes as oppressed victims (see also Barry 1979; Cole 1987). MacKinnon (1989) contends that pornography and prostitution objectify and reduce women to things, commodities, and sexual body parts for men's sexual enjoyment (MacKinnon 1989). For instance, Andrea Dworkin notes,

> Prostitution in and of itself is an abuse of a woman's body. Those of us who say this are accused of being simpleminded. But prostitution is very simple... In prostitution, no woman stays whole. It is impossible to use a human body in the way women's bodies are used in prostitution and to have a whole human being at the end of it, or in the middle of it, or close to the beginning of it. And no woman gets whole again later, after (1997, p. 141).

Andrew Dworkin (1993) firmly rejects the notion that a woman would ever freely choose prostitution, as doing so involves the self-infliction of an inhumane treatment. In denying women's consent to prostitution, she states (1997, p. 149) that, "prostitution comes from male dominance, and not from female nature. It is a political reality that exists because one group of people has and maintains power over another group of people." To Dworkin, prostitution, and sex work more broadly, exemplifies political dominance over women, and all prostitutes are victims of violence.

Such viewpoints and arguments have been drawn upon by research activists who argue that sex work itself constitutes violence against women and the sex industry as a whole should be abolished, including Melissa Farley (1998, 2004), Janice Raymond (2004), Raphael and Shapiro (2004), and Donna Hughes (2003). Based on the argument that prostitutes are oppressed victims, they seek to criminalize the sale and purchase of sexual services. These moralistic views have exerted a paramount influence in forming the general views about prostitution both in society and in academia that tend to refer to sex workers as "fallen women," "women who have lost their virtue," or "sexual slaves" (Abrams 2000; Addams 1912; Kunzel 1993).

The opposing view ascertains that sex workers are empowered, liberated women who actively make choices in order to improve their own lives, albeit in constrained circumstances. This camp of feminists argues that it is the men who feel so powerless in the presence of women's sexuality that they have to pay for women's attention and sexuality. The money men use to buy women's attention crystallizes men's confession of their weakness. For instance, Erikson and Tewksbury argue that their findings reveal that it is the women who "hold the power to establish and enforce the norms of micro aspects of their interactions with patrons" (2000, p. 292). Schweitzer also points out that women exploit the men and reverse the conventional male versus female roles (2001, p 72, see also Frank 2007). This perspective shows that it is the women who have total command over their bodies, and their association with sex constitutes the source of their greatest power.

The third view is presented from both researchers and sex workers. It intends to break the dichotomy and prove that sex workers just like workers in any other service sectors, are neither complete victims nor completely liberated women, but are in a continuum between the two extremes (Benoit and Millar 2001; Ford 1998a; Jennes 1990; McLeod 1982; Pons and Serra 1998; Shaver 1988, 1994, 1996; Almodovar 1993; Bruckert 2002; Chapkis 1997; Delacoste and Alexander 1987; Doezema 1998; French 1988; Boyton 2002; Lever and Kanouse 1998; Pyett 1998). Researchers in this camp sometimes employ their findings to argue that it is criminalization that generates working conditions that facilitate violence at sex work, and that sex work is not inherently dangerous or violent (Kempadoo and Doezema 1998; Rekart 2005; O'Doherty 2011).

The sex workers' rights movement also argues sex work is a legitimate form of labor and that sex workers need rights, not rescue (Bindman 1998; van der Meulen 2011; Chapkis 1997; Leigh 1998; van der Meulen and Gillies 2007; Wahab and Sloan 2004; West 1998). This view asserts that decriminalization is necessary in order to diminish the violence experienced by sex workers (O'Doherty 2011). As the next section will clearly demonstrate, each of these ideological stances produces dramatically different legal and public policy results.

A Politically Charged Environment: Anti-Trafficking Campaigns, Abolitionism, and Police Raids

As discussed previously, abolitionists argue that pornography, prostitution, and violence against women are of the same nature (Bernstein and Schaffiler 2004; Spector 2006; Vance 1984). Indeed, contemporary anti-trafficking, anti-prostitution, and anti-pornography activism has resulted in calls for national and international legislation designed to protect women from violence (Brown 1995). As a result of this debate, one camp opposes legalization of prostitution and argues that prostitution could never be a voluntary occupation and it is always forced and coerced because prostitution is based on systemic dominance of males over females and is intrinsically and inherently a modern form of slavery that is harmful, dehumanizing, and exploitative. The other camp promotes legalization of prostitution and argues that the stigmatization of prostitution represents a hegemonic control over women and legalization of prostitution will restore women control and agency over their own bodies (Doezema 2001).

This polarizing debate on legalization of prostitution forms the basis of the international debate on trafficking. Two international NGOs that are prominent in the anti-trafficking movement, the Global Alliance Against Trafficking (GAATW),

and the Coalition Against Trafficking Women (CATW) embody these two opposing views. While CATW argues that illegalizing prostitution is an effective way to
combat trafficking, GAATW contends that legalizing prostitution can reduce trafficking because it is the illegality of this profession that fuels trafficking-related
exploitation.

The joint U.S. governmental and anti-trafficking activist efforts around the
world take an abolitionist stance toward prostitution, in an attempt to criminalize prostitution and deny even the possibility that sex work could ever be a viable
economic choice (U.S. Department of State 2012). As the U.S. government and
others have adopted this abolitionist stance, governmental and nongovernmental,
and organizations, including the United Nations, face pressure to declare a shared
standpoint. Doing otherwise has very real consequences, as countries that do not
meet U.S. minimum standards with respect to the prevention and prosecution of
trafficking and protection of survivors not only risk losing U.S. donor funds but
may find it more difficult to obtain assistance from international financial institutions such as the International Monetary Fund and the World Bank choice (U.S.
Department of State 2012).

Fighting trafficking thus has become part of a much larger moral crusade
against prostitution (Weitzer 2006, p. 33). In the address to the General Assembly
of the United Nations in the fall of 2003, Bush proclaimed that it was the duty
of member nations to increase international cooperation against transnational
crime syndicates and increase efforts to combat the sex industry. Bush's address
conflated trafficking with the commercial sex industry as he called for combined
endeavors to abolish the "old evil" (U.N. 2003).

The Bush administration's anti-prostitution and abolitionist views have
determined who are worthy fund grantees and who are worthy trafficking victims. Through a January 2008 passage of the Tom Lantos and Henry J. Hyde
United States Global Leadership Against HIV/AIDS, Tuberculosis, and Malaria
Reauthorization Act of 2008, the U.S. government required that any foreign, nongovernmental organization receiving U.S. government funds for anti- trafficking
efforts overseas must sign an anti-prostitution pledge (U.S. Congress 2008). This
act ensured that harm reduction groups that actively engaged with sex work were
no longer eligible for funding unless they explicitly condemned prostitution as
objectionable. The U.S. Department of State's Bureau of Public Affairs issued a
fact sheet in 2004, stating "The Link Between Prostitution and Sex Trafficking,"
emphasizing that voluntary prostitution involving adults leads to sex trafficking of
women and children (U.S. Department of State 2004).

Thus, the policy required governments and organizations to endorse a pledge
"explicitly opposing prostitution and sex trafficking" as a condition of funding and
participation in various programs to prevent the spread of HIV/AIDS and human
trafficking. The President's National Security Directive on Human Trafficking
of 25 February 2003 notes: 'Prostitution and related activity, which are inherently harmful and de-humanizing contribute to the phenomenon of trafficking in
persons, as does sex tourism, which is an estimated US$1 billion per year busi-
ness per year" (U.S. National Security Presidential Directive 2003). Accordingly,

USAID notes, "Organizations advocating prostitution as an employment choice or which support the legalization of prostitution are not appropriate partners of USAID anti-trafficking grants or contracts" (Samarasinghe 2003, p.101).

The Victims of Trafficking and Violence Protection Act (TVPA) requires that the United States Department of State release an annual Trafficking In Persons (TIP) reports. The TIP reports group countries into three "Tiers" based on the degrees of compliance with TVPA standards, including efforts of prevention, protection, prosecution, and rehabilitation to eradicate trafficking. If a state fails to make these efforts to combat trafficking, the TVPA authorizes the denial of all non-humanitarian aid and threatens their diplomatic relations with both the U.S. and international development institutions including the International Monetary Fund and the World Bank (U.S. Department of States 2012).

As a result, in the fight against trafficking, the U.S. funding restrictions have channeled political legitimacy and government resources to prostitution abolitionist groups and governments. Organizations that either adopt a non-judgmental stance on prostitution or conduct peer-group education strategies to empower sex workers against discrimination and abusive working conditions have been excluded from funding. The benefited, funded groups and governments reject any distinction between "forced" and "free choice" prostitution and view eradication of commercial sex work as crucial to anti-trafficking movement and HIV/AIDS prevention programs. They increase the number of brothel raids and crack down on commercial sex establishments in an effort to convince U.S. officials of their commitment to the goals of the TVPA and a continued need for funding.

By creating incentives to abolish prostitution and promote abstinence as the only U.S.-approved approach as a means to stifle human trafficking, this international alliance has built, shaped, and perpetuated an international moral and legal order of anti-trafficking movements. As scholars have contended, some politicians have often used language about sex trafficking to describe all forms of trafficking and invoked the iconic figure of prostitutes as "modern sex slaves" to galvanize an international movement to end trafficking and the sex trade. Research that debunks the notion of "modern day slavery" and relates the anti-trafficking discourse incites a moral outrage against the sex industry, which President George W. Bush referred to as the "special evil in the abuse and exploitation of the most innocent and vulnerable" (U.N. 2003).

The belief that all migrant sex workers are trafficked victims is also built into the latest United Nation's definition of trafficking. The definition states that exploitation "includes, at a minimum, the exploitation of the prostitution of others or other forms of sexual exploitation" and that the consent of the trafficked victim is "irrelevant." Sex work is defined as a coercive form of sexual exploitation and the lived realities of sex workers are disregarded and dismissed.

By declaring that all prostitution is sex trafficking, anti-trafficking campaigns enable law enforcement officials to exercise force to raid brothels, arrest, detain, rehabilitate, prosecute, and deport women and children detected and identified as illegal migrant sex workers. These law enforcement measures are on the increase due to the US funding policies described previously.

By supporting the effort to abolish prostitution and promote abstinence as the only U.S.-approved approach as a means to stifle human trafficking, this international alliance has built, shaped, and perpetuated an international moral and legal order of anti-trafficking movements. The U.S. has taken measures such as police rescue, enforced 'rehabilitation,' and deportation of those deemed as trafficked "victims." Pressures to generate arrests and locate undocumented "trafficked" sex workers spur law enforcement officials to crack down on brothels, rather than more hidden sites of labor exploitation.

Anti-trafficking strategies of raid-and-rescue also push sex work underground and make it more dangerous. Policies condemning prostitution and promoting "rescue" further marginalize and alienate sex workers. They exacerbate the danger, exploitations, and abuses sex workers encounter, such as continued police harassment, corruption, and discrimination.[2]

Impact on Researchers: Institutional Review Board Approval

This ideologically and politically charged environment has an effect on whether sex work researchers' research proposals can be approved by the review board. Researchers can propose their sex work research but will not be able to undertake the research unless their institution's review board approves their project. Indeed, due to political policies about sex work and moralistic concerns of the review board, sex work research is often rendered a "problematic area of inquiry" and can potentially face rejection by the board (Sanders 2006, p. 451, see also Mattley 1997). Nonetheless, this predicament is not insurmountable. To overcome this hurdle, I recommend that sex work researchers familiarize themselves with the kinds of issues and concerns carried by the review board and address them in a thorough, thoughtful, and reflexive manner in their research proposals.

In terms of my own research proposal, the block I received in seeking board approval was a demand for a detailed delineation of the means through which I could protect my research subjects from being harmed by my research. In response to the demand made by the review board, I scrutinized my entire project and provided a thorough assessment of the risks and benefits my research could potentially bring to the research subjects: sex workers, clients, and government officials. In view of these risks and benefits, I explored a host of precautions and measures to minimize the risks and maximize the benefits for the research subjects. Based on this account, the review board issued an approval. As shown in my case, the review board showed no interest in learning how my safety as the

---

[2] Sex work researchers such as O'Doherty (2011) have proven with their detailed, sound research that it is the criminalization that facilitates violence against sex workers and that sex work is not inherently violent and dangerous.

researcher could be maintained. Indeed, the safety of the researcher was never a concern for the review board in reviewing my research.

While the safety of the research subjects, rather than the safety of the researcher, was the central concern of the review board in gauging my research proposal, it appears that other sex work researchers have different experiences. Indeed, different universities have different sets of protocols. For many sex work researchers, their blocks from the review board include concerns about the safety of researchers, the methodologies of researchers, and the reputation of the institution (Sanders 2006; Shaver 2005).

It is said that the review board's cultural beliefs about the sex work industry can engender their concerns about researchers' safety and possibly, ultimate rejection of the research. Sex workers are usually conceived as either good or bad women, being exploited or exploiting others. The sex work industry is often associated with deviant, illegal, and criminal behaviors, and linked with STDs, HIV/AIDS, and drugs. The people who organize, manage, and work in the sex work industry are often considered violent and nefarious villains. These cultural stereotypes can concern the review board members since researchers have to navigate and maneuver alone through the underground, illegal space. The review board members may envisage the researcher's life at great risk, and hence rejects the project (see Sanders 2006).[3]

Under such circumstances, to address the review board's concerns about their safety, sex work researchers need to elaborate on procedures through which they can protect their own safety. For instance, they can specify in their research proposals that personal interviews will only take place in public places instead of private places. They can also state that they will keep daily contact with a friend so that friend can be updated with their safety status. Other measures to maintain safety include but are not limited to: keeping a cell phone on hand at all times, always walking with a partner on the street of the red light district, knowing local conditions, choosing field sites carefully, being respectful and not threatening to sex workers and authoritarian figures, and making sure everyone knows the researcher's status as the researcher (Sanders 2006; Limón 1994; Bourgois 1995; Bernstein 2005; Agustin 2005; Shaver 2005, p. 302).[4]

In critical times during my own research, such as when I was pulled to an upstairs sex room by several gangsters, the establishment manager intervened and reminded the gangsters of my researcher's status, which prompted them to release me. My public status as a researcher saved me many times from imminent danger such as gang rape (Zheng 2009), but it was only through my participant observation in this environment that I was able to ascertain the level of risks that women faced in their work. Hence it is a matter of serious concern that some IRBs may

---

[3] Sanders (2006) discusses the predicament and indeed, the rejection, that she encountered seeking approval from the review board for her research proposal during her graduate school years.

[4] Shaver (2005) provides a long list of precaution techniques for sex work researchers to maintain their safety in different contexts, including street sex work and indoor sex work.

deem the ethnographic method of participant observation unacceptable due to the moral concerns about the appropriateness of sex work industry research or suspicions that ethnographic methods could present risks in a volatile, dangerous environment (Agustín 2005, Sanders 2006). While the collection of the data are based upon the ethnographer's observations, memories, and informal interactions and conversations with research subjects, the IRB may question the potential quality of the data and the validity of the methods (Sanders 2006).

In some cases, it seems that concerns about the reputation of the institution may cause the review board to reject a research proposal. Sociologist Teela Sanders (2006, p. 452) reports that when she was a graduate student, her IRB proposal to carry out an Internet-based survey with sex workers was declined by the review board. The board claimed that it was "an unacceptable area of inquiry and methodological design." Sanders attributed the rejection of her research proposal to the university senior officials' trepidation and anxiety about the reputation of the school, which could potentially be undermined by the media coverage of the student's unconventional project and association with the sordid world. As Sanders ascertains (2006), institutions, to protect their reputation, would either veto a project or demand modifications that could completely overhaul the research design and methods proposed.

Hence, to obtain approval from the review board, researchers need to thoroughly scrutinize the research design and fully assess the risks and benefits of the research to both researchers and research subjects, paying particularly close attention to ethical issues involved in protecting confidentiality (Stein 2010). Indeed, sex work researchers who have successfully employed ethnographic methods in their inquiries into the sex industry should serve as models for novice researchers to follow in the process of undertaking and fulfilling the study.

Impact on Researchers: Access to the Sex Industry

As the disparate and highly politicized stances on sex work have shaped anti-sex work legislation and public policy, this politically charged environment makes it difficult for researchers to access the sex industry and gather data. To overcome this predicament, I recommend that, unless researchers know the establishment manager or owner personally, they should use a third party to introduce them into the sex industry, and at the same time, make it clear to the people involved in the research that the research poses no political threat to them.

Accessing the sex industry can be difficult due to research participants' suspicions regarding a researchers' political agenda that, in turn, stems from broader issues related to anti-sex work laws, policies, and cultural stigma. As discussed in the previous chapter, many sex work researchers engage in exploitative research methodologies with anti-sex work political agenda, and produce results that further stigmatize and marginalize sex workers. Aware of this history between researchers and sex workers, many sex workers feel guarded and hesitant about participating in research projects, especially since they have no knowledge about the researchers' political stance. Establishment owners, managers, and workers are equally wary of the political consequence of their involvement in the research. To traverse the vast rift between the sex work community and researchers can be a difficult task.

If the researcher is a local him/herself and personally knows the establishment manager or owner, the mutual trust built between friends could make it far easier for the researcher to access the establishment. However, it seems very rare that sex work researchers happen to be friends of brothel owners or managers. Even in such cases, researchers have to inform their friends, in this case, owners or managers, of the research agenda and research methodologies, and request informed consent. In most cases, however, sex work researchers do not personally know establishment owners or managers.

A third party is usually needed to introduce the researcher into the sex industry, either on the street or indoors. This third party can be a person, an institution, or an organization. Examples of the institution and organization are: shelter, welfare services, healthcare institutes, sexual health organizations, sex worker activist group, sex work outreach projects, and criminal justice system such as prisons and courts (Sanders 2006). Among these organizations, researchers have noted that sexual health organizations can sometimes decline researchers' requests due to fears regarding overwhelming time commitments, ideological disagreements, and worry about possible exploitation of sex workers (Melrose 2002).

Despite these difficulties, it seems that researchers have had some success in carrying out work in conjunction with sex work-related outreach projects. These groups usually have excellent relationships with both street workers and indoor establishments. The long-term, trusting bond that exists between sex work outreach projects and sex workers has made sex work outreach projects a productive gatekeeper for researchers (Sanders 2006, p 454). In general, as mentioned, in negotiating with the third party to serve as a gatekeeper, researchers need to make their research agenda and research methodologies transparent.

With this in mind, researchers need to impart to the third party the ways in which they will protect the confidentiality of research subjects and minimize the risks and danger the research will bring to the people involved in the research. They should also explain how the data and research findings are likely to be utilized and disseminated. If the third party is a sex worker activist group or sex worker outreach project, then researchers should establish their pro-sex work political stance and the ways in which they will endeavor to use the data and research finding to assuage cultural stigma and normalize sex work (Hubbard 1999)

Once introduced into the sex industry, researchers need to be aware of their new social environment and avail themselves of techniques to build relationships, cultivate trust, and make friends. Since any kind of small blunder or misunderstanding can potentially breach mutual trust between researchers and research subjects, sex work researchers usually attempt to develop an alliance or a network with research subjects through providing help and service to research subjects, maximizing the time spent with research subjects, living and working with research subjects, altering researchers' own dress code and demeanor, forging close ties with a small number of key informants, and so on (Dewey 2011; Zheng 2009).

I will use my own example to illustrate the ways in which access and acceptance into the sex industry can be accomplished. As I embarked on my research on sex workers in China, I found a university professor who was willing to be my gatekeeper and introduce me to an establishment. I was overjoyed and intent on collaborating with him. However, it did not take me long to find out that he held a political agenda that was incongruent with mine. In my meetings with him, he handed me a list of research questions, research goals, and interview questions that he had designed, which evinced ideological rifts between us. He wanted the research to prove that sex workers were victims in need of rescue and sex work should be eradicated. Once I was aware of the disagreements of our research premises, I decided to terminate the collaboration and embark on my own search for access into the sex industry.

During this incipient stage of my research, my research and my identity proved the target of mounting suspicion from people around me. After I approached some official contacts and informed them about my research, I was suspected of being a spy sent by the United States (Zheng 2009).

Negative cultural responses to my research resulted in refusals and rejections of my research requests by every establishment owner I contacted. Government officials were also reluctant to reveal what they regarded as "secret information" to me, contending that doing so might jeopardize their own political positions. They did not even attempt to cover their suspicion of me (Zheng 2009, p. 28).

The nature of my research created barriers in my relationships with these potential research participants, although the breakthrough finally came when one of the political officials asked me to be his daughter's English tutor, and I agreed. In exchange, he introduced me to a couple of establishments to conduct my field-work (Zheng 2009).

The establishment owners attempted to use the situation to their advantage. They seized the chance to ask for favors from the official, who as a senior govern-ment official controlled municipal resources. One owner, for example, hinted that he was interested in renting a plot of land in the city center. Because of the ideal position of this land in the heart of the city's largest commercial district, bidding for the land user rights would be intense. In the end, the establishment owner him-self called off the deal, saying that he was sick of constantly having to bribe and kowtow to political officials. Likewise, owners saw me as a potential resource for their business and other plans. I was frequently grilled for information on busi-ness conditions in the United States, the best ways to go abroad, strategies for their children's education, and other matters (Zheng 2009).

Access into the establishment was only the first step to the success of the research, as I still faced the major challenge of garnering acceptance from the sex workers, building relationships, and locating those willing to participate in my research. My initial attempts to interact with the sex workers were not very successful for a number of reasons. The women's attention was squarely focused on business, and they would not talk to me. In fact, they did not even have time to listen to me, because their eyes were fixated on each entering client, and they

concentrated on the selection process. My cultural style also marked me as an outsider, and they referred to me as "glasses" and "a college student", ridiculing my student attire and my inability to understand or participate in their sex talk and jokes, and they distanced me from their circle.

The women did not believe I would be able to understand their lives, especially their inner turmoil, simply because I was not "in their shoes." They insisted that differences in experience and background would prevent me from knowing their pain, and they were extremely wary of their own security from the assaults by the police, thugs, and so on in their dangerous environment. They were also cautious in dealing with each other because any women might have some network with important people in the city that might harm them, and so each woman used a fake name, a fake hometown, and a fake personal story (Zheng 2009).

To overcome these barriers and build trust with the sex workers, I decided to increase the amount and intimacy of my interactions with them. I paid the rooming fees to the owner and lived with the women in the establishment, and thereafter became intensely involved in every aspect of their lives. I also served clients as a hostess, although I did not provide sexual services. Although it was not my initial intention to research worker client dynamics by directly servicing clients as a hostess, objective circumstances mandated that I wait on clients. Customers who saw me would naturally assume that I was a hostess, and doing so ensured that I fulfilled my obligation to minimize the disruption of my research on the normal business operations.

Working and living with the women gave me a chance to seek expert advice from the women who taught me techniques to negotiate with customers and ward off customers' sexual advances. We shared the same frustration, fear, and jokes from servicing customers, evading police raids, and escaping thugs' assaults. Sharing the same experience eventually drew us together and established a trusting bond between us (Zheng 2009).

As illustrated, due to the ideologically and politically charged environment that researchers enter into when focusing upon this subject, access into the sex industry is rarely achieved without a third party's introduction as a mediator. Successful access into the sex industry with a third party's mediation is the most crucial step in research on sex workers that opens up precious opportunities for researchers to cultivate trust and build connections with research subjects with ethnographic research methodologies.

Impact on Researchers: Danger, Risks, and Stigma

Research conducted in such a fraught environment can potentially cause psychological risks and bring stigma and marginalization to researchers. Ferrell and Hamm (1998) have used the term "edge work" to describe field research in criminal or deviant settings that compels researchers to struggle between legality and illegality, morality and deviance. Indeed, sex work researchers' experience

is fraught with danger, risk, and stigma, all of which present significant ethical challenges and concerns.

Many researchers have discussed all sorts of psychological effects that carrying out sex work research has had on them in academic works and personal essays (Bruckert 2002; Dudash 1997; Egan et al. 2006). While some researchers experience emotional distress from sex workers' stories of rape, violence, and physical abuse, others undergo emotional disturbance, confusion, tension, marginality, and insecurity. For instance, Brewis describes her sense of "horror" when listening to sex workers' accounts of sexual harassment and repeated assaults, "squirming discomfort" over accounts of certain sexual practices, "empathy" over women's experiences, "sadness and anger" regarding the violence that haunts women's lives, and "profound admiration" for the women's intelligence and spirit (2005, p. 495).

Dworkin (1981, pp. 302–304) depicts her emotional reactions of infuriation, fear, nausea, isolation, and desolation from her research on pornography. As she notes, researching pornography gives her vivid nightmares, makes her unable to trust her partners in relationships, and offers terrifying ways to envision everyday objects. Researchers clearly experience powerful emotions when dealing with the subject of sex work, irrespective of their ideological position.

In my own research, I experienced a profound sense of vulnerability, powerlessness, and anger as I witnessed my close friends being physically abused by the establishment owner, bouncer, and manager. I experienced a deep sense of fear and terror many times, especially as I was hiding with the workers in a dark room upon police raids, or as I was being dragged to an upstairs sex room by several thugs. I also felt an immense amount of frustration and depression as I was surrounded by misogynist comments about women and confronted by an utter objectification of myself. In that environment, it was my looks and my body that defined whom I was, not my mind. I also experienced a profound sense of loneliness as time passed by with no intellectual interlocutors around to make sense of my experience.

I experienced a deep sense of stigma and marginalization when my friends started shunning me, telling me that they were worried that I carried sexually transmitted infections because I was enmeshed in the sex industry. At home, I experienced a devastating sense of distress when my parents sat me down in a severe manner, degrading me and begging me not to become a "prostitute." In many ways, the effect the research exerts on me is engendered partly by the fraught environment, and partly by my own gender.

Feminist anthropology has a long history of critique underscoring how it is impossible for researchers to maintain a genderless identity in the field. As Ruth Behar notes,

> The woman anthropologist, the woman who writes culture, also has breasts, but she is given permission to conceal them behind her pencil and pad of paper. Yet it is at her own peril that she deludes herself into thinking her breasts do not matter, are invisible…[that] the male gaze does not take them into account (Behar 1996, pp 1–2).

Eva Moreno further echoes these sentiments in her account of being raped by one of her research assistants during her ethnographic fieldwork, an experience that led her to state that "in the field, one is marked" (Moreno 1995, pp 246–247, cited in Coffey 1999, p. 93). Moreno's incident tells us that it is simply not possible to enter the field as a "neutral-researcher-body," "unmarked by gender and sexuality" (Brewis 2005, p. 498).

Indeed, the way local people interpret and react to a fieldworker's gender and sexuality carries significant cultural meanings and shed light on the cultural norms of the research setting (Coffey 1999, p. 82). In my case, the stigma and marginalization I received from my friends and my family reveals cultural stereotypes that demonize and demean sex work. The overwhelming objectification of me as a woman underscores the gender inequality and patriarchal nature of the environment. The danger and risk of rape, police arrest, and abuse that I was subject to is also revealing of the volatile, violent, and precarious environment.

Witnessing my close friends being physically beaten right in front of me made me feel powerless and helpless, and overturned my initial belief that researchers have more power than research subjects. Indeed, as I remained silent accepting derogatory and misogynist comments about women, as I remained silent witnessing physical abuse of my friends, and as I remained silent listening to the stories of rape and injustice, I achieved an objective researcher's "highly disciplined subjectivity" (Scheper-Hughes 2000). My silence allowed me to obtain valuable data that helped to illuminate the myriad forces that coalesce in the lives of hostess bar workers, but, at the same time, my silence also enacted and reinforced the existent social structure.[5]

Ethical Practice of Reciprocity

Establishing reciprocity between research subjects and researchers can potentially help the research benefit participants in the work as much as it benefits those who carry out the research. Fieldwork data are gathered from long-term participant observation, interviews, and informal interactions with research subjects, with whom researchers form a bond of trust and a close relationship. To avoid exploitation of research subjects, researchers should be active in engaging in a process of reciprocity with research subjects.

I hope that my own research can serve as an example of effective reciprocity. I believe that the dissemination of my research data can potentially help inform and generate public policies and services to improve sex workers' health, ameliorate sex workers' rights issues, and challenge discriminating stereotypes and myths about sex work. Although my research results can positively affect sex workers' lives, my research process in the sex industry was not able to improve

---

[5] Irwin (2006, p 171) notes that we all "do structure" when we conduct our research and when we write. She maintains that fieldwork relationships between researchers and research subjects can reinforce gender and other inequalities, just as "experimental texts and taboo topics can support and perpetuate larger practices that perpetuate historic inequalities."

the women's economic livelihood or change their lives. During my fieldwork, I was constantly worried about obtaining more from the participants than they did from my research. The solution, as I came to find out, was to ensure a mutual reciprocity.

During my research, I did not just lend a sympathetic and neutral ear to the women's stories. I became many women's confidante and offered them advice and insights into their life and their relationships with other women and male customers. I offered health information and advised ways to protect their health. I also helped to take care of some women while they were sick, while they went through abortion, and after they were abandoned by their clients. Many women told me that they felt grateful that I was able to help them in times of need. They told me that they were thankful to have a friend, a helper, and a listener, and that talking with me was beneficial in helping them find new ways and new perspectives to understand their lives and problems.

I not only offered my confidante friendship, but also shared with the women stories about my own life that helped to build bonds of rapport while also establishing that I had some understanding of their struggles. Dewey (2011) also engaged in this type of emotional reciprocity in her work with exotic dancers by sharing stories with the women about her own working class family background, which helped to consolidate her relationships with the dancers based on a common class background. As I shared stories with women in the hostess bar, we came to realize our similarities in being filial daughters and sacrificing ourselves for our parents. Finding common grounds between us furthered our understanding of each other and strengthened our emotional ties. As we became close friends, they revealed to me their most inner thoughts and most secret stories about themselves. They took me to visit their families, see their parents, boyfriends, friends, and clients.

Some women also used their relationships with me as a Western-trained scholar as a form of social capital to raise their status in the eyes of their friends and customers. For instance, one of my informants took me to her apartment to meet her client who kept her as a mistress. She boasted to her client of my advanced study in the U.S., and her client was very impressed that she had a friend like me. According to her, the fact that we were friends elevated her worth in front of her client. Another informant took me to her rural hometown where she took me to practically all the street corners and families to tell her friends, relatives, and family members that she was going to follow me to America soon. I could see the shining envy and admiration in the eyes of her friends and relatives. I was also used as a testimony to her successful life in the city when she repeated her fake story to the people about her respectable job and economic success at a publishing house.

My own research experience demonstrates that an ethical research project necessitates reciprocity between researchers and subjects to ensure minimal exploitation of, and maximal benefits for research subjects from the research. We as researchers have obligations toward individuals who participate in our research and put our obligations into action through practice of reciprocity with those who help us with our research.

Ethical Practice of Reflexivity

Research in an ideologically and politically charged environment necessitates that researchers take a reflexive approach to the research process. It is highly recommended that, throughout the research process, researchers practice reflexivity through engaging in active, continuous, and critical reflection on the knowledge produced and the means through which the knowledge is acquired (Guillemin and Gillam 2004). Reflexivity not only ensures the quality and validity of research data, but also promotes high standards of ethics in researchers' awareness, the research process, and resulting practices.

Feminist and postmodern researchers began to demystify the discourses of scientific objectivity in the 1990s following the appearance of theoretical and methodological texts that underscored the highly subjective nature of ethnographic research (Visweswaran 1994; Moore 1995; Wolf 1992; Jascia-Lees, Sharp and Cohen 1989). These scholars argued that reality itself is socially constructed and therefore knowledge is both situated and created within particular cultural and historical contexts. Such scholarship directly challenged the authority of "grand narratives", and the process questioned whether knowledge production could ever truly hope to be objective (Polkinghorne 1988; Moore 1995).

This body of feminist and postmodern work called upon researchers to engage in reflexivity throughout the research process by including their own experiences in the process of analysis and production of knowledge. Indeed, a reflexive account of the research process is as important as the results, given that reflexivity not only ensures researchers' accountability for the research, but also reveals the cultural norm of the research setting (Hart 1998). It is important, for instance, for readers to understand how the researcher's own experiences of the field informed her (or his) analysis of it.

What kind of issues should researchers reflect upon? The following questions are just a few examples of the kinds of questions researchers should ponder throughout the research process. How does my positionality with respect to class, race, culture, gender, sexual identity, beliefs, and behavior shape my research questions and research design? How does my positionality underpin my research process and my interpretation of research data? How does my positionality impinge upon my framing of my research results? How does my positionality influence my relationships with my research subjects? How do I reduce the barrier with research subjects? How should I represent them?

To answer these questions, it is critical that researchers engage in an ethical practice of reflexivity during research and writing, to make transparent how they have come to know what they know, how their positionality shapes their relationship with research subjects, and how their values and beliefs inform their interpretation and writings. A description of the interactions between researchers and participants can help readers observe researchers' ethical negotiations and efforts to ensure participants' autonomy, dignity, and privacy.

Researchers who adopt these ethical practices expose themselves in the writing and do not conceal themselves by posing as objective, hidden authoritarian experts. While they reflect on their own social positions, researchers not only practice the belief that readers have the right to know that the knowledge is socially produced, but also empower readers to evaluate the text with their own judgment. In this way, researchers achieve ethical responsibilities and accountabilities for their writing. In my own ethnography, I explicitly place myself in the reflexive narrative and describe the ways in which my cultural position, social history, and professional role connect me in unique ways with my research subjects and how my layered identities and beliefs shape my analysis and interpretations of them (Zheng 2009).

Researchers can also be reflexive with respect to the power in the form of issues that permeate every aspect of relationships between researcher and research subjects. We can provide readers with an account of what are the ethical dilemmas we encounter during research and how we resolve them, how we negotiate relationships with research subjects, how we perpetuate power inequality in the research setting, and how we interpret and represent research subjects. Although we may be powerless and vulnerable as observers in the field, we cannot deny the fact that we do possess the power to represent our research subjects and claim the research result as our work.

Conclusion

In this chapter, I have contextualized sex work researchers in an ideologically and politically fraught environment and explored the impact of this environment upon researchers' abilities to receive IRB approval, access the sex industry, and preserve physical and psychological integrity in the field. The cultural and political issues surrounding sex work place intense and complex demand on researchers. To successfully operate in such a hostile and volatile environment, researchers will likely find it indispensible to become immersed in the research setting and continuously negotiate it with care. In this chapter, I have proposed two ethical strategies, specifically reciprocity and reflexivity, for researchers to cope with working in a fraught and often divisive environment.

As we have seen, sex work researchers are confronted by vehement debates about sex work. While one camp depicts sex workers as victims of exploitation who should be rescued, the other camp conceives sex workers as liberating and empowered agents. Despite the ubiquity of these two extreme views, more and more researchers have argued for a third position. That is, sex workers are not different from workers in other service sectors in occupying a space between the two extremes.

This dichotomized view of sex work constitutes the basis of the international debate on trafficking. More specifically, the dominant anti-trafficking campaign adopts the perspective that all prostitutes are forced, exploited victims, and all sex work should be outlawed. The campaign conflates sex work with trafficking and encourages police force to raid brothels and arrest, rehabilitate, and deport women rendered as "trafficked" victims. Based on this moralistic movement, the U.S. federal anti-trafficking stance has determined an abolitionist and anti-prostitution view as the prerequisite for organizations to receive funding.

This ideologically and politically charged environment has a profound impact on sex work researchers at all stages of research. Prior to the research, researchers face the impediment of the review board that often holds a negative view of sex work research and possibly rejects it. To overcome this predicament, I have recommended that researchers address the review board's concerns in their proposals in a thorough and reflexive fashion. More specifically, researchers should detail the ways in which they will maintain the safety of research subjects and researchers, minimize the risks to research subjects, and ensure the validity of research methods and the quality of research data.

At the initial stage of the research, researchers may find the politically charged environment impede their access to the sex industry. To cross this hurdle, I have suggested that unless researchers personally know the establishment owners or managers, researchers should elicit help from a mediator who can make appropriate introductions and facilitate researchers' entry into the sex industry. I have also provided examples of these mediators, and delineated the ways in which researchers, after their entry into the sex industry, can obtain acceptance from sex workers and build trusting ties with them.

During the course of the research, researchers may find that the fraught environment spawns danger, risks, and stigma to researchers. I have provided examples of these risks from other researchers' accounts and my own research experiences. I have noted that local people's response to researchers' gender and sexuality including stigma, marginalization, objectification, gives away the cultural stereotypes of sex work and gender inequality at the research setting. The danger and risks of police arrest and rape also unravel the unstable and perilous environment.

I have recommended the ethical practices of reciprocity and reflexivity to cope with the fraught environment. The practice of reciprocity can prevent exploitation of research subjects and make the research benefit research subjects in profound ways. The practice of reflexivity can make the researcher and research process transparent, demystify the authoritarian, objective voice of the author, and endow readers with the right to make their own judgments. The exposure of the researcher and the research process can also ensure researchers' accountability and reveal the social structure that shapes the research setting. Finally, a reflexive account divulges the ways in which researchers are restricted by, yet reinforce the cultural norm of the research setting.

Chapter 4
Between Research and Activism: Identifying Pathways to Inclusive Research

Susan Dewey, Jane S. for The Sex Workers' Outreach Project (SWOP) New Orleans & Jenny Heineman, for The Sex Workers' Outreach Project (SWOP) Las Vegas

Envisioning Participatory Sex Work Research

In a book by anthropologists, it is of course worth mentioning that much of what anthropologists do in their research is already quite participatory. Anthropologists generally live with and as part of the communities that they hope to better understand, and in this process of participant observation they ideally come to know the nuances of everyday life for individual members of a particular group. Indeed, it is not uncommon for anthropologists to share deep and sometimes life-long bonds with participants in their research, nor is it uncommon for anthropologists to feel a strong sense of self-identification with the communities in which they have become embedded through their fieldwork.

In many ways, most anthropologists are already familiar with some elements of participatory research and may even incorporate these practices into their work, irrespective of the name they ascribe to it. Yet actual participatory research takes anthropological engagement in a community a step further by actually placing elements of the research design, implementation, and analysis process either partly or exclusively in the hands of individuals who engage in behaviors or practices that the researcher seeks to understand. In doing so, the hope is that the research process becomes much more fulfilling and meaningful for all concerned.

Participatory research "...represents a convergence of principles and values... in which the community determines the research agenda and jointly shares in the planning, implementation of data collection and analysis, and dissemination of the research" (Wallerstein and Duran 2003, p. 28). Sometimes also called community-based participatory action research (PAR), action research, mutual inquiry, or feminist participatory research, its research design and methodological strategies strongly emphasize community strengths in the development of research that endeavors to solve social problems. This philosophy positions researchers and community members as equal partners in praxis, which can be defined as the process by which theory or ideology becomes realized in the form of concrete action.

Thus informed by these noble intentions, participatory research constitutes a process that begins with researchers listening to community members articulate issues around a key set of themes, which can then be used to create a structured dialogue that paves the way toward social change on the community's terms (Wallerstein and Duran 2003, p. 42). This process dates to the 1960s, when social science became much more strongly tied to activism designed to provoke and stimulate the creation of social change (Wallerstein and Duran 2003, p. 27). Yet the theory itself originated with social psychologist Kurt Lewin, who, writing as early as the 1940s and (unintentionally) anticipating many of the feminist critiques of science and knowledge production that would follow decades later, strongly questioned the positivist acceptance of empirical objectivity in social science research (Adelman 1993, p. 7).

This chapter will explore how this enduringly revolutionary set of ideas continues to provide great possibility for sex work research. By reviewing examples of successful participatory research with sex workers, we will explore the ways in which participatory research presents sex work researchers and research participants with great potential to overcome research barriers such as stigma, mistrust of authority figures, and misplaced perceptions of community needs. Participatory sex work research remains relatively rare for the same reasons that complicate other forms of research with marginalized or stigmatized populations. Some of the ethical challenges in this variety of research stem from the very real legal and emotional risks participants may face, as the preceding chapters clearly illustrate.

Researchers keen to engage in a participatory project with sex workers must proceed cautiously, but they may do so with the knowledge that such work is in fact possible and has been successfully undertaken by others. While relatively rare, participatory sex work research projects have been carried out in anthropology, public health, and related fields. Such studies have been pioneering in their use of participatory processes as a means to engage sex workers, and have done so on the premise that these processes have greater potential to engage hard-to-reach populations while simultaneously generating community-generated recommendations for change (O'Neill et al. 2008, p. 83).

With so much to recommend it as a social justice strategy, one might wonder why more participatory sex work projects have not been carried out. Participatory studies have the potential to produce pioneering results but can be very difficult and time-consuming to organize, as the ideal of building a team of like-minded researchers, sex workers, and other relevant community partners can be fraught with a number of problems. Accordingly, the following section highlights potential problems that aspiring participatory researchers may encounter as well as possible solutions to these quandaries.

All participatory research projects with sex workers must be able to overcome or at least address the reality that many sex workers live and work in a sociopolitical environment that marks them as criminals due to laws that prohibit prostitution and many related behaviors. Individuals who perform illegal forms of sex work can experience stigma that, when combined with engagement in criminalized behaviors, deeply complicates their abilities to participate in activism or other projects that could expose their sex work activities to previously unaware family, other employers, friends, other community members or, of course, law enforcement.

In thinking about the possibility of carrying out participatory work, researchers must be sensitive to these realities, including the possibility that they are asking sex workers to participate in potentially dangerous work that could result in their arrest and/or estrangement from those closest to them. This is particularly complicated for those engaged in illegal forms of sex work, including the director of the New Orleans branch of the Sex Workers' Outreach Project (SWOP-NOLA), who maintains her anonymity because of her involvement in criminalized prostitution. When she first started SWOP-NOLA, maintaining her own anonymity was her first priority and she attempted to construct a leader-less presence, hoping that, over time, a community would form organically around the idea of sex workers' rights in New Orleans, information-exchange regarding nonjudgmental social, legal, and medical services, and the ultimate goal of decriminalization and destigmatization of sex work.

For SWOP-NOLA's director, remaining an invisible presence was also an attractive goal because she wanted to maintain an inclusive environment that welcomed sex workers regardless of race, socioeconomic group, gender, legal status, and type of work done. She therefore thought it unwise to identify information about herself that may read as a bias toward people like herself, meaning those who are white, cis-female, educated, and currently working as full-service providers. While she still believes that her goal of remaining as anonymous as possible was both justified (in terms of her own safety) and wise (in regards to remaining universally welcoming to a diverse group of New Orleans sex workers), this approach was problematic for a number of reasons.

First, it is difficult, if not impossible, to gain the trust of those she was attempting to attract, as sex workers in New Orleans (as elsewhere) are by necessity distrustful not only of outsiders but often of each other. A prostitution arrest and/or conviction will almost always bring with it a heavy dose of public shaming, and until recently, the Louisiana "Solicitation of a Crime Against Nature" (SCAN) statute also carried with it mandatory inclusion on the state sex offender registry, which not only serves as a scarlet letter of those convicted, but limits access to housing, straight jobs, social services, parental rights, and many other basic civil rights (Women with a Vision 2011).

Louisiana sex workers can also often be an easy target for law enforcement when local politicians want to appear "tough on crime" or actively engaged in anti-trafficking activities (NOPD 2011). As a result, Louisiana sex workers are especially, and understandably, distrustful of anyone new. As a faceless, identityless activist promoting the brazen, pro-sex work, anti-criminalization philosophy of an organization they had never heard of, SWOP-NOLA's director was a stranger when she started organizing, and in the eyes of some sex workers, likely an undercover law enforcement agent.

SWOP-NOLA's director came to realize, over time, that the level of anonymity she was attempting to preserve was simply unrealistic, as any type of organizing and activism requires a certain level of visibility. She manages the SWOP-NOLA website, authors the weekly newsletter, communicates with prospective members, and the domain and hosting accounts are registered in her name. Though that information is protected from the public, law enforcement could demand access to it. She is SWOP-NOLA's most visible member as the advertiser and promoter for the organization, both on- and offline, she frequently distributes flyers and enters both commercial and nonprofit places of business to share information about SWOP-NOLA.

With these factors in mind, she decided to admit that she is a local sex worker doing criminalized sex work, despite the fact that doing so exposes her to criminal investigation and arrest. She realizes that this choice means that she also risks alienating local sex workers whose work is not criminalized and may not see her as someone who shares a set of common issues with them. She is constantly aware of the risk she is taking by making herself a visible activist for sex workers' rights and by promoting an organization that supports that cause. If she was targeted by law enforcement, there would be obvious repercussions to her personal life, her income from sex work, and her (hypothetical, future, non-sex work) professional career. She has decided to take these risks, aware that her privilege as an educated white woman protects her to some extent, as does her living situation. Since she is not a parent or caregiver, her potential arrest does not directly affect anyone else.

Yet despite the fact that she is confident in publicly supporting this cause while maintaining some level of anonymity, the vast majority of New Orleans sex workers whose work is criminalized do not feel comfortable contacting her or publicly aligning themselves with the organization in any way, despite the fact that they might have interest and support the cause, and can be assured that SWOP-NOLA is not working with law enforcement. These sex workers share a wariness of guilt by association, fueled not only by fear but also by a general misunderstanding of sex workers' legal rights.

The co-director of SWOP-Las Vegas has contacted the head of the metropolitan Las Vegas vice squad several times to address the abuses sex workers experience on the street at the hands of law enforcement. Several sex workers have confided in her that law enforcement routinely agrees to drop charges or not make an arrest in exchange for sexual services. For her, the most difficult part about doing activist organizing while simultaneously remaining off the law enforcement radar is addressing the major human rights abuses that are indeed happening because of law enforcement. Also, because the co-director is an outspoken person who has done numerous media interviews on the topic of sex worker rights, law enforcement dismisses her requests to work with SWOP-Las Vegas as "agenda laden." In this respect, SWOP-Las Vegas' attempt to work closely with law enforcement has unfortunately led to an even greater divide.

Both SWOP-Las Vegas and SWOP-NOLA advocate for the decriminalization of all forms of sex work between consenting adults, which would undoubtedly minimize the risks sex worker face when participating in research. SWOP-Las Vegas' co-director feels that until this lofty goal has been attained, institutions of higher learning and their respective IRBs could be more supportive of sex work research. The co-director's position as both a sex worker and sex work researcher, n her opinion, sometimes causes her to worry that her work is not taken seriously ecause of the stigma surrounding those who cross that bold line between merely esearching the sex industry and actually being a part of it.

SWOP-Las Vegas' co-director has found that moral policing within academia remains a reality that she must confront as part of her everyday lived experience as both a scholar and a sex worker. She finds this reality extremely puzzling given that she works at the University of Nevada Las Vegas, where she feels that there are probably more sex workers putting themselves through school, per capita, than at any other university. She attests that many of these student sex workers are terrified of doing participatory research in an industry they know so intimately because they are afraid of receiving a potentially negative response from their professors. They are terrified that male professors will see them as hypersexual and, alternatively, they are scared that female professors will view them "bad" feminists.

These issues make it even more essential that researchers who are not sex workers themselves remain mindful of the realities that shape sex workers' lives. SWOP-Las Vegas' co-director strongly encourages researchers to place a high value on sex workers' time, which can include providing financial incentives for participating in research. She hopes that IRBs will eventually come to understand that many of the cultures surrounding sex work frequently involve the exchange of money for social time, and researchers should not be an exception to this rule. Paying for interviews, in her view, is not coercive for sex workers and may even lead to better data, since the sex worker will be able to focus more completely on her (or his) time with the researcher rather than worrying about losing money by not working during that time.

Stigma plays a role in shaping perceptions about sex work research, just as it plays a role in some sex worker's reluctance to organize or work with other sex workers toward the goal of social change. The director of SWOP-NOLA notes that there is a definite internalized whorephobia among sex workers of all types, and this manifests itself in a number of ways, including language use. Most individuals who engage in transactional sex in New Orleans do not refer to themselves as "prostitutes" or use the word "prostitution" to describe the work they do, despite the fact that their income-generating practices may legally qualify as such. Likewise, the term "sex worker" is not yet widely used in New Orleans, as many prefer more vague euphemisms, such as escort, companion, sensual massage provider, or model.

This linguistic use speaks to the reality that sex worker community in New Orleans (as elsewhere) is a highly stratified one, though the hierarchy is somewhat subjective and dependent on the perspective of the individual sex worker. For example, many strippers consider themselves superior to escorts, but some escorts (and many—if not most—escorts who command multihour, high-cost appointments) believe the reverse. Many fetish service providers class themselves above escorts, even if they provide sexual contact up to, but not including, vaginal or anal penetrative sex, and vice versa.

SWOP-NOLA's director further notes that even among escorts doing the same work, independent providers will often consider themselves a step above those working for an agency, while those working for respected agencies may regard themselves as elite due to their association with a legitimate business. Individuals may also ascribe status to their labor based upon the setting in which they work, whether street-based, in-call (at the sex worker's location), or outcall (at the client's location). And some, including sugar babies, professional dominatrices, and providers with the highest hourly rates, might not self-identify as sex workers at all. But by and large, those who provide direct contact between themselves and clients—those whose work is criminalized—class themselves in terms of the price they command. Those who work on an hourly rate are "above" those who price each sexual service individually and up-sell as necessary; additional status hierarchies within this subgroup directly correlate with the prices commanded per hour.

In the experience of SWOP-NOLA's director, such hierarchy fosters an "us-versus-them" mentality and provokes a certain amount of resentment between those doing different types of sex work. A given sex worker may be reluctant to associate with those doing different types of work, even if they are working toward a common goal. If it is a type of work the individual deems to be "below" her (or his) own position in the hierarchy, there may be a fear of being associated with that "lower" type of work. And there is sometimes a reluctance to associate with someone doing work generally considered to be "higher" in the hierarchy than one's own, as that person may be perceived to be snobbish. Both may believe that they will not be able to relate to one another.

It is problematic that many sex workers are reluctant to organize with those doing different types of sex work or working for larger amounts of money. SWOP-NOLA's director has found that some individuals who offer highly specialized, high-priced services, and describe themselves as professional companions, gentleman's companions, or professional courtesans, for instance, may not self-identify as sex workers at all, and may consider the term off-putting or even insulting. This is unfortunate because, as may be expected, those providers commanding the highest prices generally possess a certain level of privilege that grants them access to resources that may be helpful to the group as a whole, whether that is knowledge of the law, health information, or technology, or have social connections to those in positions of power who may be able to help individuals or adult industry professionals more generally.

SWOP-Las Vegas' co-director reports that there have been similar identity-based difficulties in attempting to organize sex workers in her city. Several years ago, for instance, a movement to unionize strippers was internally sabotaged in the form of female strippers' protests against having a transwoman as the campaign's leader. The kinds of strict hierarchies between different forms of sex work, as SWOP-NOLA's director noted, come with different levels of stigma whereby people involved in sex work frequently define themselves by what they are not. This is somewhat paradoxical given that it is not uncommon for individuals to move between different types of sex work due to need or interest.

Yet despite some amount of fluidity between discrete sex work-related occupational behaviors and beliefs, these hierarchies remain firmly in place in ways that complicate activist organizing. The pervasiveness of social stigma and negative social narratives surrounding all forms of sex work makes it difficult to put the blame on individuals for failing to engage in activist organizing. SWOP-Las Vegas' co-director is a macrosociologist, which has encouraged her to view this pervasive stigma as a structural problem related to the cultural dehumanization of sex workers and widespread sexism rather than a problem with individual members of the movement consciously sabotaging it. The limited amounts of funding available to organizations or individuals involved in advocating for sex workers' rights contrasts rather starkly with the well-funded and highly organized abolitionist or anti-trafficking groups that position sex work as a simplistic problem of violence against women.

These realities result in a situation in which individuals must volunteer long hours in effort to stay abreast the latest happenings and crises. For example, an abolitionist may write a scathing op-ed about sex work advocates and then the onus is on sex worker advocates to defend their position. The unfair advantage comes from the fact that, because the anti-trafficking platform is socially and fiscally supported by the majority of philanthropists, nongovernmental agencies, and governmental agencies, they have the time, financial support, organization, and general ability to focus much of their energy toward their cause. When the onus is then placed on sex worker activists to defend their platform, they must put aside other work, volunteer their time, and attempt to find childcare that is often out of their financial reach just in order to keep the movement alive. However, SWOP-Las Vegas' co-director strongly believes that such hardships are an inherent aspect of taking an alternative path far from the status quo, a choice that can be riddled with heartache, disagreement, stigma, and loss.

In such a divisive environment, it is self-evident that researchers themselves may be the target of others' suspicions or stigma. This book has already provided several examples of researchers' successful collaborative efforts with harm reduction or other sex workers' advocacy groups. Such organizations have the potential to be instrumental in facilitating participatory research through the trust building and cooperation they may be able to foster between the sex worker populations they serve and research. By allowing researchers to engage in outreach or other activities that could bring them more closely into sex workers' worlds, these groups could ensure a more participatory approach to research.

Yet not all groups and researchers share the same vision of what constitutes research, what particular sex worker populations might want or need, the role research might play in activism, or some combination of all these things. Some groups may be wary of engaging in collaborative work because of what they see as the potential for exploitation in the research relationship. For instance, a harm reduction organization may feel that there is great potential for retraumatization, if a researcher asks sex workers to share their experiences with violence. The researcher may feel that asking such questions is necessary in order to learn about incidents of violence in sex workers' lives, thereby potentially providing powerful evidence in support of public policy and legal change. For the harm reduction organization, conversely, this risk of retraumatization only compounds other factors in the lives of their target population, and thus far outweighs the potential long-term benefits of the research.

However, as we have seen elsewhere in this book, some sex worker or harm reduction groups may be open to the possibility of working with researchers, such as the transitional housing facility for sex workers that Susan lived in during the initial stages of her research in a U.S. city. Susan brought a keen understanding of the complex nature of social services to this work, and before the research began she suggested that the facility director to draft a contract that stipulated what she would like terms of their relationship to comprise. The resulting contract clearly specified that the organization expected her to assist them with grant writing, with transporting residents to and from work or appointments, and to otherwise assist with other tasks that an otherwise overburdened and understaffed, underfunded organization could not reasonably perform. She was happy to take on these tasks, and in return she was able to spend part of each week for nearly 6 months living with the women with the understanding that any resulting publications would respect their confidentiality to the utmost.

This approach worked very well in the context of social services, where memorandum of understanding contracts, releases, and confidentiality agreements are all normal parts of everyday life for both social service providers and those who interact with them. In international contexts or in fieldwork outside of institutions, this approach would not be advisable; in fact, even requesting the signing an informed consent form in such environments may provoke suspicion intense enough so as to void the research relationship. However, there may be other more culturally appropriate ways for the researcher to agree in advance with the organization or community about the terms of their relationship. Some researchers may criticize this as naïve given that relationships in the field inevitably change with time, but Susan would argue that such efforts by researchers to approach institutions and communities with respect for their rules and their time may set a precedent for a mutually rewarding relationship.

SWOP-Las Vegas' co-director notes that, as with any kind of research, approaching a population for the sake of study has all kinds of implications, especially if researchers maintain an air of authority. She argues that those genuinely interested in listening to the perspectives of their research participants produce the best research, as one of the major frustrations in the sex worker rights movement is the continuous silencing. Sex workers may say, "We love our work!" and researchers accuse them having false consciousness; sex workers may also say, "We hate our work!" and researchers use that as evidence of sex workers' oppression. For SWOP-Las Vegas's co-director, good research comes from a researcher simply asking, "Why?" and authentically listening to the answers provided by participants.

Researchers who genuinely listen may find that sex workers love their work when they get to work alongside good friends, and hate their work when a researcher has just wasted their time interviewing them without providing any sense of mutual respect or financial incentive. Listening is a critical element of most human social interactions, and sex work research should not be an exception in which assumptions about sex work cloud inquiry. SWOP-Las Vegas' co-director, for instance, has been extremely dismayed and extremely annoyed when researchers (and others) express surprise at her educational pursuits. She encourages researchers to remember that sex workers, like all people, are a diverse bunch: mothers, fathers, students, queers, writers, independent scholars, linguistic wizards, geniuses, and lovers.

SWOP-NOLA's director observes that sex workers and those advocating for their rights and well being may resist working with researchers for a variety of reasons. There may be a perception that the researcher's presence may cause more work for those serving the community by constituting an obtrusive presence. Organizations or individuals that work in street-based sex work environments, which can present safety risks, may also feel a rather burdensome sense of responsibility for the researcher's safety. More worrisome still is the perception that the researcher's presence may complicate the relationship between those working with or advocating for the community and the sex workers themselves—a new, unfamiliar individual whose role is unclear and who may not have much in common with individuals in the community may jeopardize the level of trust the organization has earned over time.

SWOP-NOLA's director further identifies additional potential sources of resistance, including the perception that the researcher will gain more from the relationship than she (or he) may contribute to the organization. This concern could stem from general resentment toward the researcher and her (or his) privilege, whether perceived or real, or a distrust of academics due to the potential for research participants to feel othered or put on display as a result of an unequal relationship. Worse still, there may be concerns regarding misrepresentation in the researcher's subsequent publications, or that the sex worker participants in the research project may become targets for law enforcement. Resistance may also come from a generalized distrust of outsiders, based on the perception that someone who has not participated in something so widely and thoroughly stigmatized could never realistically understand what that entails.

These sources of resistance might be mitigated, SWOP-NOLA's director argues, by the researcher clearly articulating their sex work-related beliefs, assumptions, and knowledge, and by the researcher expressing a clear willingness to admit areas of ignorance and a need to learn. As has been made clear throughout this book, many sex workers have become almost accustomed to being spoken over and pushed into the role of passive objects rather than active creators of knowledge about their own communities. Researchers must enter into the research relationship with an understanding of these realities and work hard to establish a sense of equality between all partners in the research endeavor.

SWOP-NOLA's director recommends that sex workers should have the opportunity to actively correct any of the researcher's underlying premises or preconceived notions that do not ring true to sex workers' experiences. This shifts sex workers' role in the research from that of passive research subject to the more collaborative role of active, empowered contributor, and expert before the research even begins. In order for this equal collaboration to take place, researchers must be transparent about their motives and planned approach to the research process. Researchers must be prepared to answer sex workers' questions, including why they are interested in this group, and how their presence will this affect the group on a day-to-day basis and beyond. All participants should understand, inasmuch as can be envisioned from the project's inception, what the researcher's presence entails and be able to agree on a mutually beneficial level of involvement beforehand.

Likewise, SWOP-NOLA's director advises that researchers should be extremely clear about the ways in which they plan to prevent their research from compromising sex workers' safety in any way, particularly with respect to the potential for exposure to law enforcement. Research within any community necessarily means increased attention to community members, which creates serious and well-founded concerns for those engaged in criminalized forms of sex work. Researchers should formulate a clear-cut plan for minimizing the risks to sex workers, and ideally this should be done in conjunction with sex workers themselves.

SWOP-NOLA's director stresses the importance of reciprocity in research as a potential means to overcome some of the challenges inherent in research with a stigmatized population. She recommends that researchers offer everyone directly affected by the researcher's presence something of unique value to them, so that all concerned feel equally included as important and rewarded participants in the work. Such expression of goodwill and inclusion by the researcher can considerably build trust, particularly when it takes the form of something other than a straightforward financial incentive that may be read as coercive or, perhaps even worse, as a rather dismissive comment on the value of the knowledge gained by the researcher.

The difficulties most sex work researchers experience in obtaining grant funding often mean that financial incentives for participation in research are likely to be low, and researchers should be mindful of the message this sends to participants. Additionally, IRBs tend to keenly attune their focus upon the coercive potential entailed in offering financial incentives for research participation, which severely limits a researcher's abilities to offer monetary compensation unless research participants are performing specific roles such as, for instance, a research assistant on the project. Hence, rather than offering research participants 20 or, at the most, 50 dollars, which are the maximum amounts likely to be approved by an IRB, the researcher could offer access to resources that might benefit the organization or the community.

SWOP-NOLA's director strongly recommends that researchers offer the organization, community, or individuals involved in the project an active role, and ideally the research participants will decide upon this role themselves. She stresses the importance of a researcher having an existing connection to the community, whether geographical or in terms of life experience, which helps to assure potential research partners that the researcher will engage in responsible work that is of some benefit to the community. For instance, Susan frequently mentions her family members' involvement in sex work as a means to demonstrate that she has knowledge of the life that transcends research; she has also found that some research contacts in New Orleans derive some assurance from the fact that her husband is from the area. Knowing that she has at least some Louisiana roots, and that these are roots she has actively chosen, helps demonstrate that she is unlikely to engage in further othering of an oft-exoticized region of the United States.

SWOP-NOLA's director advises that researcher's willingness to share this kind of personal or intimate knowledge about her (or his) own life can help to put the researcher's academic interest into more meaningful context for potential participants in the research. Researchers who have experience engaging in transactional sex may find that disclosing this information helps to build community with research participants. However, researchers must remain attuned to the fact that their own experiences, including their experiences with sex work, may be very different from those they hope to engage in their research.

A researcher who attempts to overemphasize similarities between her (or his) life and that of the research participants also runs the risk of being condescending or disrespectful. For instance, a college-educated individual who engages in indoor sex work and is able to exercise a great deal of control with clients is very different from a street-based sex worker struggling with addiction, homelessness, and a variety of other dire life issues. SWOP-NOLA's director worries that a relatively privileged academic researcher who, irrespective of her (or his) own sex work background, may conflate her (or his) own experiences with that of someone in a less privileged position in an attempt to build rapport. Researchers must remain mindful of the significant differences in class privilege and access to resources that unfortunately remain inherent in some aspects of the research process.

Just as harm reduction or sex workers' advocacy groups may avoid or refuse to engage with researchers out of desire to protect the sex worker population they work with from the risks of potential harm or exposure to retraumatization, they may equally resist collaborative overtures by researchers due to ideological differences. The politically and ideologically charged scholarly debates surrounding sex work remain operative in activist, harm reduction, or other organizations as well, and are no less contentious in those spheres.

Some sex worker or harm reduction groups may be resistant to participatory research due to perceptions that academic research perpetuates stereotypes that position sex workers as deviants who have little autonomy. These groups may have concerns that subsequent research-based publications might highlight trauma narratives as a signal to "help" women to leave the sex industry. Likewise, groups that take an abolitionist approach in framing sex work as an unjustifiable form of violence against women may not want to work with researchers who are interested in presenting sex workers' narrative accounts of their work on anything but negative terms. It is important to mention that groups that follow a social justice or harm reduction model are not necessarily less likely than abolitionists to encourage participatory research.

Researchers who face such roadblocks may feel frustrated by what they perceive as the group's failure to see the merits of participatory research. This may even cause the researcher to doubt the merits of the project or, worse still, wonder whether a genuinely collaborative relationship may even be possible as long as the divisive political debates surrounding sex work continue to exist. It can be difficult to see room for engaging resistant communities or groups in participatory research, but such problems do have the potential to be overcome. One possible way forward might involve the researcher forestalling her (or his) enthusiastic launching into the merits of participatory research and listening attentively to what the group's or community's needs might be prior to even proposing the research. Literature reviews can surely be of great use in formulating these initial ideas, but a researcher's greatest strength may lie in intimate knowledge of the everyday workings of the group or community.

Reciprocity is always a necessity in the research process, and in this case it may ensure a productive path toward engaging in participatory work. Sex work researchers often ask their participants to reveal very intimate details, and researchers should equally expect to disclose their motivations for engaging in this work. Researchers should be prepared to discuss their motivations for engaging in this type of work as well as their reasons for pursuing a topic that often invites suspicion of the researcher's own experiences with or perspectives on sex work (Manderson 1992). For instance, sex workers' advocacy groups may not be interested in collaborating with a researcher who has not had direct experience working in the sex industry, whereas those researchers who openly disclose previous engagement in this type of work risk incurring stigma or other negative professional outcomes as a result of their choice to disclose this information.

Researchers must tread very carefully in thinking about how they wish to engage in participatory work, what it might involve, and how they intend to overcome such obstacles. It may be a good idea to observe relationships between groups and individuals that are particularly involved in sex work-related issues in a given community. Paying close attention to existing difficulties, fractiousness, or other problems can provide researchers with a sense of what potential for collaboration may exist, and which groups or individuals might be best positioned to fully participate in such work.

Susan learned many, many lessons as she attempted to forge allegiances with sex worker advocacy and harm reduction groups when she started a new job near a U.S. city with which she had very little familiarity. In thinking about the possibility of engaging in participatory sex work research with groups in this community, she dramatically overestimated how involved she might be able to become with some groups and underestimated the potential for collaboration with others. She began scheduling the meetings with the belief that harm reduction organizations would be the most interested in a participatory project, especially those that regularly engaged in outreach activities with street-based sex workers.

Susan based her estimations of her chances of success on shared similar commitments to harm reduction and desire for direct engagement with sex worker populations. However, she could not have been more wrong; in fact, she experienced enormous support from a faith-based organization that she had initially discounted due to her own underlying (and, in retrospect, extremely biased) assumption that a faith-based group would emphasize the "wrongness" and immorality of sex work. She assumed that such a position would alienate sex workers by positioning them as sinners in need of redemption. To the contrary, working with a faith-based group provided her with the opportunity to see the prominent role that faith played in some women's recovery from addiction and traumatic experiences, many of which preceded their entry into sex work.

Researchers should actively endeavor to interrogate their own assumptions about the ideological stances held by groups when they begin to conceptualize the possibility of carrying out participatory research. Likewise, researchers must think critically about the populations with which they wish to work and the multiple and sometimes divergent needs among individuals within that population. Sex workers vary enormously in their motivations for engaging in this type of labor, and researchers must be cognizant that individuals may want very different things. For some, sex work is a more lucrative income generation choice undertaken from a number of other options that seem less appealing or more time-consuming, whereas for others it is the only survival strategy available to them due to precarious housing status or education. Some individuals in the latter group may have aspirations and needs that may be better served by a faith-based group that emphasizes love, support, and personal transformation in a community environment that resembles a large family living in a single home.

However, this is not to say that all faith-based organizations operate in such an inclusive and non-judgmental way because, as with individuals, organizations can have wildly variant missions and goals. The following example is useful because it counters stereotypes about ideological dogmatism and underscores how researchers may encounter unexpected resistance for reasons that may never become clear. During one preliminary meeting Susan scheduled with a self-identified harm reduction group, she had barely settled in the chair and introduced herself before the director abruptly interrupted to ask, "Susan, I know you want us to work together, but first we need to know, what are your politics?" A bit surprised by her response, Susan answered rather obliquely by talking about harm reduction and her faith in the participatory process, which seemed to satisfy her.

Nevertheless, Susan's subsequent efforts to engage failed, with phone calls and emails unreturned. She still occasionally sees members of this group at harm reduction meetings in one of the cities where she is carrying out research and they are friendly to one another, but clearly this group did not envision collaborative work with Susan as part of their organization's goals. Despite her failure to form a relationship with this group, Susan still believes that transparency and accountability are in order when attempting to forge alliances with sex worker or harm reduction groups, which can understandably be suspicious about motives. Susan teaches in Gender and Women's Studies, which seemed to spark some concerns, among groups she met with early in her research as potential collaborators, that she might be an abolitionist attempting to infiltrate their work. She always brought copies of her publications with her to assuage this concern, as her work has always been respondent-driven and, she hopes, fairly balanced in nature.

At a minimum, researchers in a U.S. context should expect that sex worker advocacy or harm reduction groups will likely want to understand the researcher's position on decriminalization and the stance that she/he has taken in previous publications or in formulating the initial research design. Sharing this material openly may help to minimize risks of ideological conflicts later in the research process, but it may also abruptly derail any possibilities of collaborative research. Sadly, such is the reality of carrying out work in a criminalized environment characterized by divisive political debates that are, in turn, informed by ideas about morality.

A related issue in terms of ideological conflicts stems from the reality that researchers' own perspectives on sex work-related issues may change, or become complicated, as the research progresses. For instance, during pilot work Susan carried out on street sex workers' notions of risk, many of the research participants were women struggling with addiction and homelessness. It became very difficult, at times, for her to clearly see choice and agency with respect to women's sex work-related decision making, particularly as the women described lives in which the need to acquire money to buy crack cocaine (the drug of choice in the area where Susan carried out the research) and a night in a motel room prompted some women to engage in sexual behaviors that they felt caused them harm and distress.

Working with women who described sex work as their only option for earning money dramatically complicated Susan's previous understanding of sex work as a form of labor. Her ideological stance derived largely from her research with dancers, some of whom did escort work, held that sex work is real work. She shared this position with most of the women who participated in her dancer research, as the majority acknowledged that while they would rather work in an environment less clouded by stigma, dancing presented a legal and relatively safe option for income generation that also included flexibility and increased time to spend with children (Dewey 2011).

Engaging with women who used sex work as a primary means of facilitating their drug addiction presented an entirely different and infinitely more complex picture. They were women who would be limited in their ability to engage in sex work in legal, regulated environments due to poor health and, in many cases, regular patterns of interaction with the police. The women Susan worked with in order to better understand notions of risk among street workers lived lives replete with danger from every angle. For them, violence, addiction, and abandonment were pressing everyday realities rather than the abstract discursive tropes that justify anti-trafficking campaigns discussed previously in this book. Yet some of their lengthy arrest records on charges ranging from drug possession to assault complicate a vision of victimhood as oppressed and innocent. These were women who lived violent lives in order to survive, and victimizing others was sometimes a part of ensuring their own survival.

From Susan's research with such different sex worker populations, she came to understand that the environment in which sex work is carried out constitutes a critical element of how individuals experience it. This proved particularly troubling for her because she had spent so much time in her previous research listening to dancers disparage women who engaged in prostitution, which may have been one of the ways that the women negotiated working in a stigmatized occupation. Ruby, a street-based worker Susan spent a great deal of time with during the course of her research on risk, was just as dismissive of dancers and what she called "high class escorts" as these groups generally were of street-based workers. She explained how she avoided regular clients and the affective labor entailed in maintaining such relationships, preferring instead to keep the sexual transaction anonymous:

Look, when I'm out there [on the street] I keep it business. All those girls who get all dressed up in high heels and shit, I think that's bullshit. I'm there to get my 40 bucks, get my dope, and go back to my [motel] room. I stay away from regulars, and I'll tell 'em- "I'll give you a blow job, but I'm not about to pretend I enjoy it."

Ruby's wholesale dismissal of what she perceives as the performance-like aspects of more lucrative types of sex work underscores that she has no illusions about her motivations for engaging in street-based exchanges. Her directness resembles arguments in support of envisioning sex work as a form of labor like any other, as she speaks to her refusal to engage in affective work with clients. However, a researcher would be remiss in failing to recognize that, for Ruby, all sex work-related earnings convert within a matter of minutes into crack cocaine and an overpriced, dilapidated motel room.

The wildly divergent experiences of dancers, who earn an income in a legal environment, and women like Ruby, who live in a world of illegal activities with a high risk of arrest, speak to the need for aspiring participatory researchers to think very critically about what "sex work" will mean in their research. In envisioning sex work as a continuum of behaviors and beliefs associated with the exchange of sex or sexualized intimacy for money or something of value, researchers must be careful to strive for participation that represents these very different sets of experiences and life practices, a topic discussed more fully later in this chapter.

Researchers must prepare themselves for the possibility that their perspectives on sex work may change in the course of their work. It became very difficult for Susan, in the course of her time with street-based sex workers, to understand how the lives of women struggling with addiction and homelessness might be improved if sex work were legal. For these women, sex work was just one aspect of a complex matrix that rendered them socially invisible through their addiction, lack of a permanent address, gender, and, for many, criminal record.

The more time that sex work researchers spend thinking about and developing participatory research, the more it can become very difficult to negotiate fraught ideological ground characterized by very rigid opinions which sometimes do not reflect human realities. In Ruby's case, for instance, it is difficult to locate evidence in support of arguments that view sex work as a potentially empowering choice, just as it is hard to see how adopting an abolitionist perspective that opposes sex work as a form of violence against women might help to fully understand the complex behaviors and beliefs that inform her decision-making processes.

Sex work researchers bear near-constant witness to the inadequacies inherent in polarized ideological stances that do little more than simplify the nuanced lives of individuals involved in any form of sex work. Doing so forces researchers to constantly reassess where lines might be drawn between activism, scholarly inquiry, and the emotional allegiances inevitably developed in the field. This book's introductory chapter opened with an ethnographic vignette regarding Susan's own attempts to engage in "help" provision with Kristi, a woman who in every possible way self-identified as desperate and in need of assistance to find housing, addiction treatment, and perhaps above all, a place to feel safe.

Over time, Susan's interactions with Kristi and many other women like her paralleled the experiences of many other ethnographic researchers in that their conversations rarely felt like a one-sided exchange of information. Susan got to know social service providers that the women frequented, and was often invited to participate in addiction treatment and other therapeutic meetings that the women called "group" as shorthand. One day she expressed hesitancy when invited to an addictions group by Aaliyah, a street-based worker and the social worker leading the group, who knew each other well. "Sure, I been addicted to cigarettes and caffeine" Susan explained in what she hoped was an honest and meaningful expression of ethical concern, "but what if everybody in there feels weird that I haven't felt the same things they have?"

Aaliyah raised her eyebrows and made the kind of lengthy eye contact with Susan that some women from the Southern United States use to express disbelief in a way that words cannot. Then she shifted her gaze to the social worker leading addictions group while casually tilting a violet acrylic nail in Susan's direction. "I'm just gonna lay it out here for you, because she is obviously in denial" Aaliyah said, "Girlfriend here uses her job to cover up her own pain, that's her addiction. She works all the damn time, then she comes here and stays with us."

Aaliyah's razor sharp assessment of Susan's own inadequate coping strategies highlight her keen abilities to understand others, but they also speak to the humanity of this kind of research. Many of the street-based workers who were in addiction recovery or interested in enacting some kind of significant change in their lives fully expected that Susan would do the same. Sometimes these expectations took forms that made her distinctly uncomfortable, especially when they involved religious conversion, which quite a few women used as a source of inner emotional strength. Kristi had been clean for about 4 months when she asked Susan if she believed in God. Susan shrugged, trying to avoid having the conversation, but Kristi pushed further. "I know you've had some real bad things happen to you in your life and you've known some real bad people" she said as Susan tried to avoid eye contact, "but did you ever think that maybe God wanted those things to happen so that you could come here and understand us the way you do?"

These kinds of weighty conversations dramatically informed Susan's fieldwork with street-based sex workers, and they continue to cause her discomfort because so many of them come very close to a form of autoethnography that readers might misconstrue. Yet she has chosen to include them here both because they ring true in the environment of self-transformation that addiction recovery entails every bit as much as they speak to the deeply human bonds that researchers can form in the field. It is impossible, and probably inadvisable, to avoid forming human connections with research participants.

Researchers must always remain mindful of their role in the participatory research process, even as they inevitably form bonds with individual participants in their work. Sometimes these bonds endure in unexpected ways that can haunt the researcher who wonders if she/he could have acted in another way to produce a different, more favorable, outcome in the life of a research participant. Anthropologist Steven VanderStaay (2005) describes the rapidly devolving emotional turmoil caused by his choice to lend a relatively small amount of money to a participant in his research, who used the money to buy drugs and then murdered a man in an ensuing dispute.

"Anthropology is not social work" (2005, p. 371), VanderStaay rightly observes, while simultaneously commenting upon the complex nature of human relationships that develop during fieldwork. It would be naïve for researchers to think that they may somehow excuse themselves from the politics that surround sex work, a fact underscored multiple times by other examples presented in this book. Events may transpire in completely unexpected ways that even the most rigorous of IRBs could not have predicted. For instance, when Susan was working in Armenia on a project that explored the intersections between international organizations and local cultural realities as manifested in responses to sex trafficking, she developed a close bond with a woman who had been forced into prostitution in Turkey.

The ensuing series of events, which have been described elsewhere (Berrett 2011; Dewey 2008), involved her false arrest and prosecution as the leader of a trafficking ring, and Susan's terrified flight from the country. Susan is fully cognizant of the fact that these events would have transpired irrespective of whether she had been present to witness them, but she will always be haunted by the possibility that she could have somehow done something that might have prevented this from taking place. This guilt may stem partially from the academic arrogance that comes from researchers' abilities to interpret events after the fact in a way that tells the story in a particular way. Yet there is also the human reality that seeing those close to us suffer hurts us as well.

For these reasons as well as many others, participatory research must be open to the possibility for points of view to evolve among all concerned from its inception. Part of participatory research's potentially transformative power lies in the research team's ability to reflect critically upon these changes at all stages of the research process. If ideological stances on sex work are so firm as to block certain lines of inquiry, truly participatory research may not be possible at all. Likewise, researchers may not be able to overcome their own biases regarding one perspective or another and, in some cases, may not even realize that such a bias exists until much later in the research process.

This raises the question of whether it is possible for individuals with different ideological stances to work together productively, especially in the highly politicized field of sex work research. SWOP-Las Vegas' co-director believes that individuals with differing ideologies can and often do work together toward the goal of social change. She is unwavering in her stance on decriminalization because she has seen, firsthand, the negative—even lethal—effects of criminalization. However, that is not to say that she will not work with people who have different perspectives, as she has tried on numerous occasions, without success, to engage in collaborative work with the Las Vegas Police Department.

SWOP-Las Vegas' co-director argues that while parties may have significant differences of opinion regarding decriminalization, law enforcement and activists must begin thinking critically about how to eradicate human rights abuses, specifically sex trafficking. She contends that decriminalization would enable this kind of collaboration by enabling sex workers to work closely with law enforcement without fear of arrest and even potentially requiring sex workers to report suspected human rights abuses, such as trafficking, without fear of arrest. With respect to ideological differences within a research setting, SWOP-Las Vegas' co-director recommends that instead of focusing upon divergent moral and ideological viewpoints on sex work, the real question potential collaborators should ask themselves, and each other, is: "How can we ensure our fellow citizens are the safest and happiest they can be?"

Indeed, she argues, the foremost question that should be in the front of every researcher's mind is, "How can I best represent this often silenced group such that my research will increase the quality of their lives?" SWOP-Las Vegas' co-director does not believe that a researcher who is opposed to decriminalization will necessarily produce flawed or problematic research. In fact, she knows many sex workers who do not advocate for decriminalization and hence does not believe that everyone must necessarily subscribe to the same political or ideological agenda. This further underscores the importance of listening. If a sex worker tells a researcher that she (or he) is opposed to decriminalization, the researcher should ask, "why?" Researchers must remain consistently attuned to the question of "why", especially as their research agenda progresses and they begin to critically reflect upon the results.

[margin note: sometimes there is a choice to be silent]

SWOP-NOLA's director also actively encourages researchers to reflect upon their own perceptions and the potential for their research to further perpetuate stereotypes as deviants, victims, and "fallen women" in need of rescue. The academic literature is already replete with such examples, particularly due to the fact that most sex work research is concentrated in the fields of public health, with a resulting focus on disease and addiction, and criminal justice, which positions sex workers as perpetrators. Before formulating the research questions, researchers must be completely honest with themselves about their own ideological stance, and prepare for rejection by organizations or individuals based upon this stance.

Researchers should ask themselves a number of questions regarding their perceptions and preconceived notions about sex work. SWOP-NOLA's director recommends that researchers engage in self-interrogation on some of the following key issues in order to determine which, if any, preconceived notions may cloud the way they record, understand, and interpret the experiences sex workers describe: Do you see every sex worker as a victim, irrespective of how she (or he) describes her (or his) experience of sex work? If so, are only female sex workers victims, or are male sex workers victims as well? Does this apply to cis-gender[1] and transgender sex workers alike? Do you believe that all sex workers are doing this work by choice? Do you believe that sex work is an expression of past trauma? Reflecting upon these questions can help a researcher to better prepare for some of the challenges that she (or he) will potentially face.

---

[1] Gender studies scholars Kristen Schilt and Laurel Westbrook (2009, p. 440) define "cisgender" as "individuals who have a match between the gender they were assigned at birth, their bodies, and their personal identity".

In contrast to SWOP-Las Vegas' co-director, SWOP-NOLA's director feels that researchers should endeavor to engage in participatory research with an organization that shares their goals and ideological perspectives. If researchers find that they are working under assumptions that are not consistent with the beliefs and experiences of those agreeing to contribute to the researcher's project, they should either find a group that more closely resembles and endorses their ideological stance and work with them instead, or they must start working to deconstruct and re-examine those beliefs. It is not the role or responsibility of the research participants to deconstruct that for the researcher, and it is unethical for the researcher to use the time, energy, experiences, and narratives of those agreeing to work with her (or him) to reconcile problematic or conflicting beliefs. More simply put, it is highly inappropriate for a researcher to use, whether unconsciously or not, research participants to work out a researcher's own emotional preoccupations or hang-ups.

Sex workers (especially those who trade sex for money) are a uniquely stigmatized group in that almost no one in society—not even sex workers themselves—is immune to the very basic cultural belief that sex work is low, dirty, immoral, shameful, and corruptive to society, and by extension, so are sex workers. SWOP-NOLA's director advises that anyone looking to work directly with the sex worker community should first put forth the effort necessary to closely and thoroughly examine her (or his) own attitudes toward and ideas surrounding sex work. Simultaneously, however, researchers must recognize that sex workers do not form a monolithic community, even among those of the same gender, socioeconomic status, geographical location, and type of sex work.

As in other communities, among sex workers there are philosophical, political, ideological differences, prejudices, and race/gender/sexuality-based bigotry. While ideological stances within the sex worker community vary, the researcher's ideological stance should not be in opposition to the majority of those with whom he/she is working. Researchers should not maintain a strong moral opposition to, for instance, decriminalization, if the vast majority of sex workers participating in the research believe that decriminalization or legalization of sex work is the best option for the community.

The spirit of equality framing participatory research emphasizes an inclusionary approach that bridges a number of socioeconomic inequalities. This "by the community for the community" ethos is noble, but researchers must always be mindful of exactly what they are asking of participants in terms of time, energy, and commitment to the project. Susan once had a long-time member of the decades-old sex workers' activist group COYOTE explain to her, "I can't tell you how frustrating it is to have poured every single cent I ever made and every ounce of energy into this cause, and then to see how easily abolitionist academics can mobilize support for their cause."

This sobering assessment, which she made toward the end of her activist career, referred in part to the large amounts of research funding available from the U.S. Department of Justice and other federal sources carry out research on trafficking, all of which explicitly forbids not only research on sex work but also the explicit use of the term. All U.S. federal agencies require that researchers refrain from the use of the phrase "sex work", which the U.S. Department of State notes involves "the use of language to justify modern-day slavery, to dignify the perpetrators and the industries who enslave" (U.S. Department of State 2006).

In this environment, sex work research of any kind constitutes a deeply political act for researchers and participants alike. Yet it would be a terrible mistake to assume that all research participants have equal access to resources, time, and the ability to speak openly and freely. Participatory research must acknowledge that the academic participants generally carry out their research as part of their salaried and relatively stable jobs, while sex worker participants do not. While partnerships are admirable endeavors, the participatory research team must work hard to assure that dialogue remains open despite these inequalities, and that, as much as possible, all parties benefit equally from the process.

This raises a critical point about participatory research that presents a keen ethical dilemma for those who work with criminalized sex worker populations. Engaging in truly participatory research with individuals who participate in illegal activities presents multiple forms of jeopardy to participants and researchers alike. We have already acknowledged that participants should be paid for work that they put into the project, just as their academic counterparts receive salaries and accolades for engaging in such work. However, U.S. researchers who receive federal funding cannot include sex workers or organizations that advocate for them as beneficiaries or partners in any capacity. This severely limits the potential for participatory research with particular funding mechanisms which, not inconsequentially, present researchers with the greatest potential for receiving significant funds to carry out research in responsible, long-term ways.

This participatory dilemma may be slightly easier to resolve than those presented elsewhere in this chapter. Many sex work researchers and sex worker activists are united in their goal of harm reduction, yet their respective professional missions generally benefit them in significantly different ways. Sex work researchers also have the ability to move independently between a number of worlds due to the greater power and privilege that comes with professional status, university affiliation, and any number of other ties and connections that sex workers themselves are rarely able to achieve, least of all in the United States. It would be a mistake not to acknowledge this from the inception of a participatory project.

Researchers interested in participatory projects must be sure to establish a strong rapport with the groups or individuals involved and endeavor, inasmuch as possible, to ensure that sex worker participants are paid fairly for their work. It is true that some sex worker activists work from a passionate political position that might encourage them to engage in participatory research without payment because of their knowledge that it is for the greater good, but researchers must not unintentionally abuse this goodwill by not facilitating any form of compensation, whether monetary or otherwise. Doing so only compounds the already significant differences between researchers and research participants that participatory research aspires to overcome.

All parties must work together to ensure against the abuse of time or energies, particularly when there are significant economic disparities among members of the research team. For instance, a participatory project team lacking significant grant funds might consult creatively with one another about other ways that the project might benefit all members equally. It is not enough to make vague statements regarding "potential benefits for the community", as all participants are well aware (or should be) that the academics involved are likely to benefit disproportionately in such a situation through publications, tenure and promotion, and receipt of future grant funds.

In the case of a genuine absence of funds, all members of the participatory team must have an honest conversation about the team members' goals, which could help to identify other forms of compensation. Sex worker participants who, for whatever reason, may be seeking alternate forms of employment, might benefit from having an official title as a project team member to list on resumes and in job interviews. Co-authoring publications might be another way to facilitate compensation, as might joint presentation of the project and its results to community or scholarly audiences. No matter how restricted a project might be in terms of funding, there is no excuse for team members to be unequally rewarded.

This raises the question of whether participatory sex work may be idealistic in the sense that it presupposes that all parties can benefit from the project, when in reality it is likely the researcher who will benefit the most. Researchers must consult with participatory research partners regarding what would constitute fair compensation, whether monetary or otherwise, for sex work research participants who are actively involved in project design, implementation, and the analysis of results. Likewise, researchers must actively enquire about some of the ways that everyone involved in the project, from sex worker partners to sex workers interviewed to the researchers, could feel that their involvement in the project has benefitted them.

SWOP-Las Vegas' co-director finds that participatory research may be idealistic in the sense that little funding exists for research on the sex industry unless the proposed research approaches the issue from an abolitionist standpoint, and is thus a difficult task. However, she argues that "idealism", at least as it refers to creativity and innovation in academic research, can produce better, and perhaps more inclusive, results. Designing participatory research necessarily involves innovation, particularly when working with a marginalized group.

SWOP-NOLA's director contends that while the idea of participatory sex work research is idealistic to some extent, it is not unrealistic. It is very important for researchers to consider what they are asking of those they want to include in their research; for instance, inclusion should not involve the expectation that participants will work for nothing. Researchers must realize that fairly compensating participants for their time is important, but it is also not enough, as researchers stand to gain far more from the participatory enterprise than do sex workers. Potential benefits for researchers include publication, recognition, career advancement, and all the personal, financial, and professional benefits that entails. These are lasting rewards that offer many returns: for most researchers, well-received publications lead to a position, which leads to funding to do further research, which leads to full professorship, a higher salary, tenure, and the privilege of time to focus on more research.

The sex workers who contributed their perspectives, their time, and narratives of their experiences, as well as made space in their personal and professional lives for researchers, should leave with more than a few dollars in hand. An economist does not need to engage in a cost/benefit analysis in order to determine that individual researchers will undoubtedly profit disproportionately from the exchange as compared to individual sex worker research participants, and this fact should not be ignored, and the importance of this inevitability should not be minimized. However, open communication among those involved in the research enterprise can help to ensure that the researchers are not the only one who benefit from the work.

The researcher, SWOP-NOLA's director contends, should be able to provide something of unique value to research participants in addition to appropriate monetary compensation for participants' time. Researchers likely have access to certain resources and opportunities that are not available to research participants, such as grant writing skills, connections to lawyers willing to do pro bono work or knowledge of where to find low-cost or pro bono legal services, assistance in navigating the application process for certain social services, and, of course, public or academic recognition of participants' work within the project if participants regard this as a desirable outcome. There should be some discussion before research begins, and an agreement on what participants should receive. This will obviously vary depending upon the community in question, and likely between the individuals within the community, but perhaps a consensus can be reached. If not, then researchers should work to accommodate the wishes of as many members as possible. Above all, everyone should feel that the exchange is mutually beneficial, and that the benefits they receive justify the effort they are contributing to the project.

SWOP-NOLA's director encourages aspiring participatory researchers to remain mindful of the significant risks that sex workers take in speaking to anyone about their work. Outsiders, especially those coming from a place of relative privilege, draw attention to sex workers' activities, and could potentially do so in ways that cause unintended harm. In addition to the fact that participants can never be completely sure that the researchers' subsequent publications will neither misrepresent them nor put their safety or income in jeopardy, researchers' simple presence and the attention it attracts can potentially jeopardize an individual's anonymity, income, and safety by exposing them to law enforcement or other sources of harm.

One of the most pragmatic aspects of participatory research involves a keen sense of the need to engage community leaders and other local authority figures. In every community, there are individuals who should be approached when thinking about the possibility of participatory research; it would be extremely unwise, for instance, to neglect meeting with a leading representative of a community's sole public health facility in designing a participatory project about sex workers' health. Yet doing so may be difficult for a number of reasons, the foremost being researchers' lack of knowledge of the intimate politics that sometimes characterize community and activist networks around contentious social issues.

Participatory researchers can unintentionally become embroiled in local and organizational projects as a result of their collaborative undertaking, and it can be difficult to carefully navigate this environment. Researchers must be cognizant of the complex terrain they are entering into when contacting individuals who have decision-making authority in the community, especially when the researcher is an outsider who may be unaware of local community nuances, especially regarding normative communication and other cultural practices. Sex work is incredibly context-specific and intersects with a dramatic number of factors that include the way that individual sex workers experience gender, race, and class in a particular environment. Local leaders accordingly prioritize issues as they see them, and participatory research with an outsider may, unfortunately, be at the bottom of the list.

Researchers also need to always remember that authority figures, whether in the form of a community or organizational leader, police chief, or shelter director, are incredibly busy and have much more important issues to attend to than the possibility of a research project that they may not have the time or energy to fully consider as a transformative endeavor. Researchers may face difficulties in determining just how many polite cancellations of meetings and unreturned phone calls or emails constitute an unequivocal "please leave me alone".

We are all fortunate to live in a time in which email and social media facilitate rapid connections with others we may believe share our goals, but this only goes so far. It is unreasonable to expect that leaders of groups who have historically faced multiple forms of structural violence and marginalization, some of which have contemporary forms, will leap into enthusiastic action in response to an email from a researcher they have never met before. Whenever possible, potential participatory research partners should meet in person in order to determine their shared goals and visions for what the project might entail.

Researchers can dramatically improve their chances of partnership with community leaders through thorough investigation into the organization's goals, past projects, and history of collaborative work. Simultaneously, though, researchers should also remain sensitive to the reality that individuals in positions of decision-making authority have their own motivations for not wanting to participate in research of any kind. This may never become entirely clear to the researcher, but sometimes a lack of response or resistance to a project idea can itself be revealing. Tenacity can prove efficacious in some instances, but researchers must be mindful of the fact that they are likely to encounter resistant authority figures in another context later in their research. As a consequence, the need for respect in all forms of communications is paramount.

SWOP-NOLA's director cautions researchers to remember the uphill battle being fought by those who work with (and advocate for the rights of) highly stigmatized groups, especially on a nonprofit schedule and salary. It is difficult to garner sympathy for the cause of sex workers' rights in a social environment where many individuals find humor in jokes featuring violence against sex workers, victim-blame sex workers who are victims of physical or sexual assault, and find violent crime more palatable when the victim is a sex worker. Sadly, as has been pointed out several times throughout this book, sex workers themselves sometimes perpetuate whorephobia without a second thought through their reinforcement of rigid hierarchies between different forms of sex work.

Researchers, SWOP-NOLA's director notes, must recognize that those who work in the nonprofit sector advocating for sex workers' rights have significantly more work to do than those who advocate for other important, but more widely attractive causes, such as the eradication of breast cancer or even homeless animals. Hence those who work with sex workers are, almost by default, working against the wishes of the overwhelming majority of the public, and doing so with a marginalized, exceedingly underserved group. The resources available for this cause are limited and especially difficult to secure. In other words, authority figures in this context are especially overworked and overburdened, and they are undoubtedly all too familiar with offers of "help" from misinformed individuals assuming the organization is one involved in sex worker rescue/rehabilitation, or from others who would like to convince them to adopt that approach.

In this context, SWOP-NOLA's director argues, leaders in sex workers' rights organizations may not have the time or energy to arrange to meet with researchers attempting to engage them in discussions regarding a potential project, even one that may be mutually beneficial. Some of the difficult realities inherent in their everyday work may mean that even if they are interested in the project itself, they may not have the time, resources, or energy to accommodate even the least invasive and most amicable of researchers. SWOP-NOLA's director advocates that researchers initiate their communications with authority figures by specifying what the proposed research can do for the organization. Persistence is often effective, as an individual may foresee a future time when she (or he) will be able to participate in the project. If it becomes obvious that that authority figure either lacks the time for or the interest, it might be efficacious to proceed with the project and then inquire again later, when the research has further progressed and there is perhaps something solid to present. Once there is demonstrable evidence that the work being done is in accordance with their ideological stance, goals, the authority figure may be more open to discussion and collaboration.

With a view toward potentially engaging sex workers in a participatory research project, SWOP-Las Vegas' co-director advises researchers to engage individuals in their own space and on their own terms. She advises sharing cigarettes if the researcher is also a smoker, or bringing condoms and lube to street-based sex workers. Researchers should pay careful attention to dress and comportment so as not to overtly distinguish themselves from others in that particularly social context and, most importantly, avoid asking questions that would be offensive in any other social context, such as whether individuals have been sexually abused or otherwise traumatized. Some sex workers have been harmed in this way, just as some researchers have been.

For SWOP-Las Vegas' co-director, it is important that a researcher maintains a sense of humor and honesty about their feelings and, above all, that researchers engage participants as human beings first and sex workers second. Researchers should not be afraid to share their feelings, including any potential discomfort, which can help build rapport. Sex workers can tell, almost instantly, when researchers (or people more generally) harbor some kind of need for status or validation, as many sex workers spend a great deal of time analyzing people. Above all, though, researchers must clearly demonstrate their fundamental willingness and desire to listen to sex workers' words.

A final concern with participatory research is specific to tenure-track researchers who face considerable pressure to produce publications and obtain external funding in support of their work. There is a paradox inherent in participatory research in that while it can be incredibly rewarding and transformative, it is also extraordinarily time consuming. Building the kind of rapport that allows for participatory research involves honesty and openness that can only come with time. As noted previously in this chapter, it is unreasonable for researchers to expect community members or organizations to throw an enormous amount of energy into participatory research with little to no guarantee of return. Instead, researchers must respect and acknowledge that they are interlopers in an environment in which they are outsiders in many ways. Even if the researcher has previous sex industry experience, her (or his) privileged role as a researcher mitigates this fact since the option to disclose this remains just that: an option.

Due to time-consuming nature of participatory research, tenure-track academics might consider waiting until after they have received the stability accompanying tenure before they carry out participatory research. Due to these time constraints for tenure-track faculty, it is advisable, in many instances, for researchers to carry out more conventional research studies with some participatory elements before attempting a purely participatory project. Post-tenure researchers might reasonably expect to have the luxury of increased time to develop the bonds and relationships necessary for successful participatory research.

Sex workers and sex worker advocacy or harm reduction groups will likely examine a researcher's motives for wanting to engage in collaborative research, which in itself may considerably slow down the research. SWOP-Las Vegas' co-director notes that she, like many other sex workers involved in activism, is attuned to these motivations, and would be highly skeptical of someone who had previously engaged with rescue-based organizations. She advises aspiring participatory researchers to share their real-life experiences with those they would like to engage in their work, including their own belief systems. Many sex workers understand feminism as a negative set of ideals that simultaneously demonize and pity sex workers, so researchers may be advised that while self-identifying as a feminist is important, it is abolitionist feminism that has subsumed popular discourses on sex work in recent years.

SWOP-NOLA's director would also carefully consider a researcher's motives for engaging in participatory research, including whether their interest amounts to little more than careerist pursuit of a "hot" academic topic. In thinking about the possibility of a collaborative research relationship, SWOP-NOLA's director would appreciate a researcher who had a history of working with marginalized groups through the lens of Gender and Women's Studies, and would also, as in any working relationship, be more open to working with someone who does not come from a privileged background. This lived experience of poverty and its associated hardships, she feels, would make a person less inclined to profit from her experiences.

LA's director points out that she began doing sex work because she
¦e the stress of her financial situation, food insecurity, lack of access
¬d growing debt. Sex work provides her with financial security she
has never before experienced, making the benefits far outweigh the very real risks
to her safety and health. In the case of more privileged researchers, she suggests
delegating research responsibilities to individual community members who can
better relate to and work with other research participants in the community.

The preceding list of potential problems and proposed solutions may make the
possibility of participatory sex work research seem like a distant dream for idealistic researchers. Participatory research with sex workers is possible, and the following three sections accordingly build upon the literature and years of discussions
with sex worker groups/activists to elucidate what a participatory approach to sex
work research might look like throughout all the stages of the research process,
from design to implementation to dissemination of the research results.

Participatory Research Design

All participatory research begins with the need to define the community that will
serve as the central focal point of analysis in the project. Participatory research
defines community as: "a unit of identity…a sense of identification and emotional
connection to other members, common symbol systems, shared values and norms,
mutual (although not necessarily equal) influence, common interests, and commitment to meeting shared needs… [and this research] builds on strengths and
resources within the community" (Israel et al. 2003, p. 55). A community can have
physical parameters, such as a neighborhood, or behavioral components, such as
women who engage in escort work, but it must be clearly defined and bounded in
order for researchers to design an effective project.

Although defining a community may seem like a relatively simple task, ideas
about who belongs and who does not present serious challenges with respect
to sex work, which remains a contentious phrase decades after its founding.
The struggle in participatory sex work research is to see community in a group
so divided by hierarchy and dismissive rhetoric that can sometimes mirror and
equally wield the stigmatizing power of those who malign sex workers. Many sex
workers have keenly developed hierarchies based upon what particular individuals
will or refuse to do for money. Susan has met many topless dancers, for instance,
who draw a sense of dignity and a self-identity as a worker from the fact that they
do not engage in illegal activities and have limited amounts of physical contact
with clients. Likewise, street sex workers may malign women who prostitute at
truck stops as dirty, diseased, and engaging in foolhardy risks by engaging in sex-
for-money exchanges in closed quarters often located in remote areas.

There is also an economic component to the difficulties inherent in defining sex
worker communities, as it can be difficult to see community with sex workers who
are, after all, in competition with one another for business. The widespread use of

internet-based services as a means for sex workers to meet clients has increased this competition through dramatic diversification of the types of sexual services available. In a rather ironic twist, this higher level of Internet-based visibility also promises greater anonymity for escorts who advertise there. Some escorts have elaborate screening requirements that would make it difficult for law enforcement officers to make an arrest, or to identify a person based upon the photographs available on the site, as these very rarely show a full facial view.

In some ways, the Internet provides the protection of anonymity, but it may also cause isolation. Escorts who advertise online may never meet another escort in person, and the online forums that exist for sex workers to exchange information are often divisive and client-dominated in ways that can make it difficult to ascertain community bonds. This is also true of street-based workers, particularly those who are struggling with precarious housing, addiction, or mental health problems. Street-based workers certainly know one another and rely on each other for support, but their ability to do so is complicated by the illegality of their work and the depth of their other life issues.

In this almost all sex work labor environments, stigma also works hard to fight against the creation of unitary goals. During Susan's work with dancers, many women strongly felt that they were performing a temporary role that they would shed once something better or more lucrative came along. "Well, I'm not going to be doing this forever" was an expression she often heard as a way of justifying anything from unfair wage standards to poor treatment by clients (Dewey 2011). Such an environment offers little promise for a sense of community based in a common work identity. Sociologists Barbara Brents et al. (2009) document similar patterns in Nevada's legal brothels, which feature a high degree of organization in which disproportionate power consolidated in the hands of owners and managers actively discourages unionization.

Stigma further prevents some sex workers from seeing their sexual labor as a form of work, further contributing to an environment that is in every possible way conducive to divisiveness. SWOP-Las Vegas' co-director, for example, reports struggling at times with the term "sex worker". She recalls using this term in one of the Midwestern strip clubs where she worked to the horror of her colleagues, who exclaimed "We're not hookers!" This raises a broader question, of great interest to both social scientists and sex workers, regarding the meanings ascribed to different identities, the salience of these identity labels for particular individuals, and which groups or individuals have the privilege of assigning these identities.

SWOP-Las Vegas' co-director points out that there are two sides to this inquiry into identity markers: self-identification at the micro-level and critical thinking about why people identify (or not) particular ways at the macro-level. She respects her colleagues who do not self-identify as sex workers, and notes that the pervasiveness with which sex workers define themselves by the behaviors and beliefs that they do not practice speaks to the pervasive stigma that shapes their lives. It takes a considerable amount of privilege to be able to self-identify as a sex worker and cheerfully proclaim allegiance to "the community." A person who dances naked to feed her children has a much different relationship with the terms "sex worker" and "sex work community" than, say, a PhD student who directs a local nonprofit for sex workers.

SWOP-Las Vegas' co-director observes that the shame and stigma associated with sex work is compounded for people who are already marginalized with respect to gender identity, sexual orientation, race, class, religion, and other important life factors. She believes that all people working in the sex industry face similar and considerable challenges that connect them on some level, including police brutality, economic struggles, social stigma, threat of violence, inhumane working conditions, and the potential for exploitation due to their status as criminals. However, it is extremely important to respect how individuals who engage in transactional sex self-identify. To this end, it would be most useful for researchers to ask who self-identifies with what markers, who does not, and why is this the case?

SWOP-NOLA's director thinks that it is possible to talk about a "sex worker community" only in the broadest terms and context, as she is reluctant to include exotic dancers and phone sex workers in the same category as those who, like her, do escort work, as she feels that it is problematic to imply a similarity of experience between individuals who face such significantly different challenges and dangers. She has even heard others extend the term "sex worker" to include burlesque dancers, which she finds insulting due to the implied co-optation of struggles unique to criminalized forms of sex work. When SWOP-NOLA's director uses the term "sex worker", she generally uses it to refer to someone who engages in physically intimate forms of transactional sex, including escorts or others providing penetrative sexual contact.

However, SWOP-NOLA's director also classifies as sex workers strippers and other participants in the sex industry, as some strippers occasionally engage in escort work. There are some elements of sex work that she finds ubiquitous, regardless of the type of sex work an individual chooses, and, for this reason, she find it useful to broadly categorize sex work based on legal status. Criminalized sex work falls under the legal definition of prostitution and includes the work of escorts, street-based sex workers, and some fetish service and massage providers, and legal sex work includes stripping, phone sex, and pornography. She feels that the differences in experience, risk, and relevant issues experienced by criminalized and legal sex workers are so disparate that it is rarely useful to include both under the umbrella of "the sex work community," unless there is a specific connection being drawn, such as the frequency with which individuals crossover between different forms of transactional sexual behavior.

Yet just because community is a bit difficult to define with a marginalized, stigmatized population does not mean that it is impossible. Participatory research design can define community by engaging in a series of steps intended to ascertain the group's perceptions of its own boundaries and normative practices. Israel et al. (2003, p. 60) note that participatory approaches to research design must begin with the critical questions of who represents, influences, and has decision-making authority within the community of interest.

Clearly, it is not the role of the researcher to define community where none may exist in the eyes of its members. After all, the label "sex worker" comprises a broad umbrella of behaviors and beliefs surrounding the exchange of sex or sexualized intimacy for money or something of value, and not all individuals who engage in these behaviors and beliefs self-identify with this term. Surely, "sex worker" is a useful umbrella label because it unites many different types of labor into one group that presumably has some common interests, but unfortunately there are so many hierarchies that exist among sex workers depending on what they do, where they work, and who they work with. However, as highlighted previously, it can be difficult for researchers to ascertain exactly who comprises the community, particularly as sex workers' activist groups have been criticized as "middle class" in morals and approach due to their leaders' generally higher levels of education and other forms of privilege (Whelehan 2001).

SWOP-Las Vegas' co-director, however, argues that the leaders of any social movement are typically well educated in contemporary socio-political discourse as a consequence of their relative privilege. The privileged people of any social justice movement need to listen to their less privileged members, which she feels the sex workers' rights movements has done successfully. She contends that the role of stigma ensures that there is no such as thing as a "middle class sex worker" given that no matter how much income an individual may earn, such a person still lacks healthcare and, if the work is criminalized, remains susceptible to deportation, incarceration, exploitation, and public shame.

An abolitionist feminist once told SWOP-Las Vegas's co-director that whore-shaming does not exist, which filled her with deep sorrow as she recalled all of the police reports she and others had filed, only to be told that she would not be taken seriously because of her work. Rejection by family members and non-commercial partners are realities she faces even with the amount of privilege she enjoys as a white, highly educated, cis-gendered woman. She finds it extremely curious that abolitionists and, indeed, abolitionist academics that write about the sex industry, are not held accountable for their privilege in the same ways as sex workers.

SWOP-NOLA's director finds that "sex worker" is a useful umbrella when discussing the experiences of individuals who work in the sex industry in the broadest sense. Like SWOP-Las Vegas' co-director, she feels that sex workers working in a number of sex industry venues in some major American cities interact more with one another and constitute a shared sex worker community with common interests, challenges, and concerns precisely because of their increased interaction with one another. The sex workers' rights movement, in the form of organizers and advocacy groups, has a longer history and larger presence in cities like New York, San Francisco, and Chicago. This situation in New Orleans, where different types of transactional sex remain far-removed from one another, is quite different, resulting in less unity among sex workers.

New Orleans sex workers who provide higher levels of sexual contact through criminalized forms of sex work do not, in the experience of SWOP-NOLA's director, interact with individuals working in lower-contact, legal forms of sex work. Part of this stems from the varying levels of stigma that surrounds different forms of sex work. Strippers are an excellent example of lowered levels of stigma due to the increasing popularity of pole- or exotic dancing classes geared toward women who do not intend to seek sex industry employment, more measured media portrayals, and the emergence of neo-burlesque performances. Yet the exchange of sex for money remains highly taboo; in fact, when a non-sex-worker voices his or her approval of exotic dancing, the justification is often "it's all an illusion—it's not like she's actually having sex with the customers."

When SWOP-NOLA's director worked at the strip clubs on Bourbon Street, the popular mantra was "I'm a dancer, not a whore." It is not surprising, then, that exotic dancers, who enjoy a modicum of acceptance by the general public, may want to distance themselves from escorts and other high-contact sex workers for whom the public still holds an almost universal disdain. Similarly, while there have been a few recent positive media portrayals of highly paid escort women, such as *The Secret Diary of a Call Girl* or *The Girlfriend Experience*, media portrayals of street-based sex workers are universally negative and dehumanizing. This reflects the reality that it is not uncommon for indoor sex workers (those providing full service) to regard their street-based sex worker counterparts in much the same way exotic dancers view escorts.

Despite these hierarchies, SWOP-NOLA's director finds that it has become more difficult to categorize the work of exotic dancers in New Orleans as "low contact" in recent years. Ten years ago, most clubs on Bourbon Street actively discouraged contact between dancers and customers; while dancers were allowed to touch customers (as long as they avoided the genital area), customers were not allowed to touch dancers. The most intimate act a client could purchase at that time was a $20 private dance, in which the stripper danced on a small pedestal in front of the seated customer for the duration of one song. SWOP-NOLA's director witnessed a manager scolding a dancer for "acting like a whore" during this routine activity when she placed her hands on a customer's shoulders; in contrast, high-contact lap dances are the norm today, with entire areas with special booth-type seats designated for that purpose.

According to several dancers with whom SWOP-NOLA's director is personally acquainted, the customer's expectation is that the lap dance will involve the dancer stimulating the customer's genitals with her body, and it is not abnormal for a customer to ejaculate during the dance. There is even a product, which advertises itself as the "liquid lap dance", meant to heighten the sensation and likelihood of orgasm for the (male) customer and to prevent the resulting ejaculate from soiling his clothing. In this way, the line between the work of criminalized sexual service providers and legal strippers is becoming less and less distinct, and the challenges that both face are becoming more and more similar.

In New Orleans as in other cities, sex workers tend to group and define themselves based upon shared venues, resources, customer base, and legal status. Hence fetish service providers and escorts participate in many of the same online networking and client screening sites, and interact with each other, either by necessity or by choice, much more than they might with sex workers doing other types of work. This segregation, as in other areas of social life, also occurs along the lines of gender, sexuality, race, and socioeconomic status, and it is rare in New Orleans for cisgendered female sex workers to interact with male or

transgender-female sex workers, despite the fact that they may be doii
work. Homophobia and/or transphobia may play a role in this self-segr
it also stems from the absence of necessity, as cis- and transgendered :
do not generally share the same clients and hence do not need to form alliances for
protection from dangerous clients or law enforcement, do not advertise in the same
places, and do not maintain web presences on the same sites.

Researchers may define a sex worker community in a number of different ways
that may be of salience to research participants, including type of sexual labor,
geographical location, or legal status. However defined, this must make sense to
participants in ways that they feel their beliefs and life practices receive appropriate respect. An ideal participatory sex work project in a given geographical area
would strive for equal representation, with the diversity of behaviors, lifestyle
practices, and beliefs encompassed in the phrase "sex worker" emphasizing the
need for research design that strives to encompass the continuum of sex work and
involves greater participation by individuals who perform different kinds of sex
work and thus experience their work in very different ways.

Most sex work research studies are quite specific to particular types of sexual
labor, and this may be deceptive in the sense that conclusions from data about
condom use with clients and other sexual partners among a group of high-earning
escorts who work and advertise independently may not necessarily be relevant to
women who engage in transactional sex from motels or cars as a daily means of
survival. While all of these women might be classified as "sex workers", there is a
significant difference in their life circumstances, access to resources, and ability to
engage in decision making about their futures.

Researchers must accordingly endeavor to equally represent sex worker populations, as their findings may be extrapolated to sex worker groups in which these
findings are irrelevant or are not applicable. Hence, researchers could potentially encounter problems in a participatory research study that involved dancers,
escorts, and street workers as equal partners working together on a study. SWOP-
Las Vegas' co-director recommends that researchers be extremely specific about
the demographic characteristics of the population that forms the intended focus of
the study. It may not, in her opinion, be productive to disrespect individual self-
identification and the reality that a highly paid escort and a street-based worker
have little in common, in the interests of forcing these two disparate groups
together into an overarching notion of sex work.

SWOP-NOLA's director likewise envisions a number of potential problems that
could emerge from a researcher's attempt to involve different types of sex workers into a single participatory study. These include potential resistance to working
together by sex workers involved in different venues, due to a fear, real or perceived, of guilt by association. Similarly, sex workers may resist working together
due to a perceived lack of shared experience or lack of identification due to type
of work done, gender, or socioeconomic status. For those who have grown accustomed to working alone, such as independent escorts, or in direct competition with
coworkers, such as exotic dancers, it might be difficult to share duties equally and
to recognize the validity of others' ideas and input to the project. For all of these

reasons, a participatory research project involving different types of sex workers might encounter problems in retaining participants for the duration of the project.

Yet engaging in participatory research with different types of sex workers is not necessarily impossible. SWOP-NOLA's director suggests that aspiring participatory researchers employ the same tactics that one might use when dealing with any diverse group that must work together toward a common goal. This process might begin by having individuals work together in small groups in order to identify mutual interests and concerns, comparing and contrasting personal experiences and interests. This type of exercise could be useful in that it encourages individuals to draw connections between their own experiences in the industry, while becoming familiar with the unique skills each member can contribute to the project, and it encourages working relationships that may help to keep individuals connected to their fellow researchers/participants for the duration of the project.

Following the development of a clear sense of community and its boundaries, the next step in participatory research design requires an assessment of community needs. These will vary depending on how community has been defined in the initial phase of the research design, so that if the "community" comprises escorts, the researcher will undertake a needs assessment survey with that particular category of sex workers, ideally by meeting with a range of escorts who have different experiences and positions within that occupational category.

Yet "community" can also be defined more broadly to encompass roles played by all residents in a given area. For instance, criminologist Maggie O'Neill and social scientist Rosie Campbell conducted a participatory sex work research project in the large English industrial town of Walsall at the request of a local public health organization that had received numerous complaints about street-based prostitution. Residents felt that this activity diminished their quality of life significantly and presented risks to their overall sense of health and well being. O'Neill and Campbell began the project with an overview of prostitution-related law and policy and consultation with community members, after which they trained a group of community members to help conduct focus groups, participant observation, to engage in environmental mapping of street-based prostitution activities, and to lead an arts-based workshop on the subject (O'Neill and Campbell 2006).

Consultations with community members included sex workers, residents (some of whom were sex workers), local organizations, and social service providers led the researchers to determine that street-based workers faced high levels of violence, much of which they did not report to the police, and had mixed feelings about their work. Residents who did not engage in sex work ranged widely in their opinions of and beliefs about sex work, ranging from tolerance to fear and anger, as well as disappointment in law enforcement officials' failure to deal with prostitution in a way that reduced risks of harassment and higher levels of crime that the residents felt accompanied street sex work. Overall, study participants recommended the creation of a prostitution tolerance zone to regulate the activity in a contained area as well as increased support for street-based sex workers who wanted to pursue alternative avenues of employment or to obtain assistance with addiction-related problems (O'Neill and Campbell 2006). These key participatory element of this study emphasize the reality that "communities are not marked by homogeneity but by contingency and diversity" in both life practices and opinions (O'Neill 2007).

Two rather pioneering examples of participatory research design processes come from the Canadian province of Ontario, where prostitution is decriminalized. In the first, Gender Studies scholar Emily van der Meulen made the rather unusual decision to carry out participatory research for her dissertation by working with a sex worker-run organization known as Maggie's/The Toronto Sex Workers Action Project. With extensive experience as a labor organizer and activist, van der Meulen began her research with a strong desire to "find a way that research and knowledge production could be turned into a beneficiary community project" (van der Meulen 2011, p. 371). Her "insider" status directly facilitated her ability to engage in participatory research, particularly as she was asked to join the organization's Board of Directors just as she began to think seriously about her dissertation topic.

Van der Meulen held numerous meetings over a 6-month period with sex workers who were affiliated with the organization, and the group generated the topic of labor organizing and labor standards. The group decided that the research should focus specifically upon how sex workers were impacted by the prostitution-related sections of the Criminal Code of Canada (van der Meulen 2011, p. 377). Interview questions were decided upon collaboratively with the Board of Directors, all of whom were current or former sex workers, with the understanding that interviewees would be given the opportunity to review their transcripts prior to analysis. The participatory research team did this "since research on sex work has frequently denied sex workers their own voices" (2011, p. 378).

While this project proved a success, Van der Meulen freely acknowledges that "were I an 'outsider' researcher with no relationship to the community, it is possible, even likely, that sex workers would have decided not to participate in the study out of fear that I would use the research results to argue that all sex industry worksites are exploitative and should be abolished" (2011, p. 379). Her experience speaks to the importance of having established trust relationships with community members prior to the inception of participatory research, particularly if the researcher must complete the project within a set timeframe.

Medical anthropologist Treena Orchard, like Van der Meulen, also undertook her research in the Canadian city where she lives and works, which proved an enormous asset in building rapport with the organization that she partnered with in her research. Beginning with the premise that much less attention had been paid to the experiences of women living and engaging in sex work in smaller and medium-sized Canadian cities, Orchard partnered with the director of WOTCH-My Sister's Place, a London, Ontario-based transitional support house. The organizations' clients include a range of women, approximately half of whom are sex workers, who are living with and are currently experiencing homelessness, mental health issues, and violence.

Orchard and her collaborators designed the resulting study, The Women's Inspirational Sex Work Project (WISP), with the preliminary set of exploratory goals organized loosely around trying to determine the organization of sex work in London and women's experiences of engaging in sex work of various kinds. From this preliminary data emerged the need for a focus upon improving service provision to sex workers, while simultaneously strengthening sex workers' capacities to participate as equals in the research process. This collaborative project is a model of how thoughtful participatory research design can potentially benefit multiple constituencies, which in this case included sex workers, social service providers who interact with them, and the broader scholarly community (Orchard 2012).

Participatory research design necessarily includes careful attention to methodological strategies, but the mechanics of these strategies may evolve once they are put into practice in the field. The following section discusses the methodologies employed by successfully completed participatory research projects with sex workers.

Participatory Methodologies

As with participatory research design, participatory methodologies aim to foster full community involvement inasmuch as possible while striving to gather empirical data that will be of use to the community and other researchers. Participatory research projects can vary in the amount of involvement community members have in the project, so that some projects actively involve community members in the design of the project, while other researchers design the project themselves and then recruit a community-based research team to design an effective methodological approach. The following examples of successfully completed participatory research with sex workers underscore how such studies can incorporate as much or as little participation as the researchers feel is likely to be productive.

A good example of a fully participatory project that incorporated community members from its inception is a Vancouver team-based public health project led by Kate Shannon. This project employed an innovative mixed methods approach that combined the strengths and energies of the Women's Information Safe Haven (WISH) Drop-In Center Society, which has contact with approximately 200 street-based sex workers per night, over half of whom are of First Nations or other indigenous ancestry (Shannon et al. 2007).

This community-based inquiry approach, known as the Maka Project Partnership, began with a needs assessment survey carried out among women attending the drop-in center, and findings led to a project design with research and service components, with the latter focused upon the development of activities including peer outreach and wellness workshops to be designed based upon the project's research findings. A community advisory board developed by the researchers hired, trained, and supported a team of women with experience engaging in street-based sex work (Shannon et al. 2007).

This team facilitated all focus group discussions, assisted with social mapping exercises in which street-based sex workers marked a map of Vancouver with areas where they work and their knowledge of service provision and risks in these areas, and time–space sampling that focused upon repeated and random visits to areas where street-based sex workers congregate. Using these methods, 205 research participants were recruited for interview participation along with a 6-month follow-up interview and HIV testing at both instances by a trained nurse who provided pre- and post-test counseling. Results indicated that street-level sex workers require interventions that focus upon their health and safety in order to reduce their risks of HIV and other health-related harms (Shannon et al. 2007).

In another public health study with a focus upon HIV risk, epidemiologists Kristen Clements-Nolle and Ari Bachrach worked with the San Francisco Health Department to study HIV prevalence in the San Francisco transgender community, which included sex workers. Clements-Nolle and Bachrach designed the study themselves with the end goal of understanding and describing HIV risk in ways that did not reflect simplistic gender binaries. The coresearchers understood that they needed the active participation of the transgender community in order to implement a project that could recruit transgender participants and speak to them on their own terms. To this end, they recruited 10 transgender volunteers to develop and carry out 30 interviews and 11 focus groups with a total of 100 transgendered persons, in addition to 4 months of ethnographic community mapping in areas with high numbers of transgendered persons (Clements-Nolle and Bachrach 2002, pp. 335–337).

The volunteers were supervised by a community advisory board, comprised of 24 transgender individuals recruited through social service providers and street outreach, which met bimonthly to assist with the design and implementation of the study. The board supervised the hiring of transgender research associates and reviewed pilot data findings to assure that the project was sensitive to the needs of the transgender community. When the study was complete, the volunteers presented the results to the transgender community, social service providers, and various government agencies (Clements-Nolle and Bachrach 2002, pp. 335–337).

Medical anthropologist Treena Orchard's WISP study, which was participatory from start to finish, employed qualitative interviews with sex workers and social service providers at a day shelter to explore both parties' views and experiences with respect to interpersonal and structural violence against sex workers. WISP recruited 26 worker interviewees from day shelter participants, with interviews loosely guided by questions regarding their experiences with violence, help-seeking, and service provision. To ensure that the project was community-based, WISP recruited four of the interviewees as peer workers and worked with them to develop four information sessions to achieve objectives of enhancing their abilities as researchers (Orchard, personal communication).

WISP also formed an advisory committee in these meetings and used their experiences to create a working best practices document to share with other researchers, service providers, and sex worker groups on community-based research with sex workers. Particularly in providing a deliverable at the end of the project that enriches community abilities to engage in future work, Orchard's project constituted a model of what future participatory research with sex workers might look like. The research constituted a form of community-based inquiry whereby Orchard worked hard to establish mutually respectful collaborative relationships with other organizations, and ensured that interview participants felt safe and respected in the interview environment (Orchard 2012).

Social work scholar Moshoula Capous-Desyllas (2011) employed a rather unique participatory methodology with sex workers in her use of Photovoice, an arts-based qualitative method pioneered by public health scholars Caroline Wang and Mary Ann Burriss. Implementing the Photovoice methodology requires researchers to give participants cameras in order to document, in whatever way they see fit, issues of significance to their community. In doing so, Photovoice aims to promote dialogue about community issues through discussion of the photographs, which often revolve around a social problem of interest to policymakers and community members alike. By representing difficult issues in visual format, Photovoice can work to facilitate social change by bringing "willing, powerful members of a community together with highly stigmatized people and enable the former to assist the latter by first learning with them" (Wang et al. 2000, p. 82).

Using the Photovoice approach, participants are able to define issues and frame the most relevant social action on their own terms, which means that it can serve as a form of needs assessment in a way that reaffirms community strengths and resilience. Caroline Wang contends that this is particularly useful in research with stigmatized or marginalized communities that may otherwise experience needs assessment surveys or other forms of research as reinforcing "a sense of impotence, inferiority, and resentment" (Wang et al. 2000, p. 90).

Capous-Desyllas initially encountered significant difficulties in recruiting research participants for her Photovoice study, and describes her strategies for overcoming this hurdle at length in her dissertation (2010). She was able to eventually recruit 11 female sex worker participants using a number of methods that could also be useful to others working with hard-to-reach populations. She posted flyers describing the project in dressing rooms and bathrooms at exotic dance clubs and in the lobbies of social service agencies, including a outreach centers or drop-in shelters for people experiencing homelessness, a methadone clinic, and also shared these flyers through street outreach activities with a community organization.

Capous-Desyllas also mailed letters to social service providers who work with sex workers, posted an electronic version of her research flyer on sex worker social media sites and email listservs, and announced the study on the radio. After 2 months, she still had only three potential participants and decided to advertise the study further in the newspaper, which proved successful. She provided individual training sessions to each participant, and displayed the results in a community art show as well as in her dissertation (Capous-Desyllas 2011).

The preceding sections illustrate how difficult it can be to implement participatory research and methodologies, but researchers can overcome these challenges by focusing on the sometimes narrow gap between what a researcher and her (or his) community partners envision as an ideal participatory project and what is actually possible due to funding constraints or resistance from one or more angles. Yet the participatory process is not over once the project is complete, as researchers must endeavor to distribute their findings in ways that are meaningful to the community.

Participatory Dissemination

The act of participatory dissemination comprises a number of potential steps covered in the ensuing section, including collaborative writing, community involvement via sharing of data and expertise, publishing findings in particularly inclusive ways, and project evaluation. The ways in which researchers choose to share their data and make their findings available is just as important as other aspects of the participatory research process, as findings cannot be of great use to the community if they remain confined to academic journals or other relatively inaccessible venues.

In beginning to think about options for dissemination toward the end of a participatory research project, team members must think carefully about what audiences they want to benefit from their findings and target their writing accordingly. It is highly desirable for participatory researchers to publish in multiple venues in order to reach as wide an audience as possible, but they should bear in mind while writing that this will inevitably be very time-consuming. A top tier journal in the social sciences or public health requires work that takes time that rewards researchers in very clear ways in the tenure and promotion process, but newspaper articles or other popular media reach larger numbers of people and hence have a greater potential to exercise influence.

Once data are ready for analysis in the form of interview transcripts, completed field notes, or other products gained from implementing particular methods, it is ideal if research participants and the researcher can work together to analyze the data and generate themes for writing together. This may not be possible due to lack of (participant) interest, funds, or time, in which case participants should at least have the opportunity to review the research results prior to publication. This is complicated, surely, for those who do not carry out their research, but publish, in English. At a minimum, it would be most useful for researchers to include participants in the writing process as they move toward completion.

Researchers should provide participants with some guidance when they review data or materials ready for publication, as academic writing in particular can be dense and alienating for those who are unfamiliar with this style. Developing a list of questions for participants might help them to assess whether they feel that the researcher has presented an accurate and fair depiction of their lives and whether the researcher should consider alternative perspectives. Researchers might list these questions on sheet of paper with plenty of space for writing, or meet in person to talk about them if oral communication might be a more effective means of discussing these issues.

Researchers could also engage in participatory writing with sex workers who engaged in the research as participants or facilitators, or who may not have participated in the research but still can offer special insight as a result of their lived experiences. Some of the most interesting sex work research has been published either by sex workers and academics together as part of an edited volume (Dewey 2011; Kempadoo and Doezema 1998; Ditmore et al. 2010; Van der Meulen et al. 2013) or by academics who previously engaged in sex work, as most academics will have "aged out" of sex work by the time they are able to publish (Egan 2006; Frank 2002).

Such publishing endeavors help to break down the divide between "researcher" and "subject" by actively including sex workers' voices as equal partners in the knowledge generation process. Doing so subverts the hegemonic and ultimately artificial divide between "the experts", academics who study and understand sex workers' worlds from outside following their acquisition of time-consuming and often expensive education, and "the research subjects", sex workers who are only deemed authorities because of their behaviors, which they are asked to reveal for the purpose of the research.

Researchers can also share their findings in ways that do not involve publications, such as through sharing data and expertise gathered in the course of the research. This might work particularly well for researchers affiliated with organizations that provide direct services to sex workers, as the researcher could potentially bring new ideas or ways of thinking about the organization that could improve service provision. Researchers could also offer such organizations assistance with grant writing or other areas of interest to the group. As part of Susan's agreement with a transitional housing facility that provided shelter and services to women leaving sex work, for instance, she promised to assist with program improvement based upon her observations. Doing so allowed her to be an active and contributing member of their community as opposed to a researcher "taking" data from it.

In many ways, participatory researchers are well-positioned to offer free or low-cost expertise to organizations as part of a mutually beneficial exchange (Goodman 2001, p. v). Susan played an active role in grant writing with a transitional housing facility where she carried out preparation for future research by living there on weekends. She also filled in as an extra (and, of course, unpaid) staff member who would take residents to appointments, the grocery store, or other places that an overworked staff could not. Being able to spend long periods of time with the women often provided her with many rich opportunities for thoughtful conversations that helped her to gain a deeper understanding of the particularly local dynamics involved in sex work.

Sometimes research findings can be shared in unexpected ways that function to build rapport with research participants. One breakthrough moment at this facility occurred when Susan was spending the night (on a futon in a back office, so as not to deprive anyone of space) and a few bored residents were using Google to search for information about various people they knew. They then chose Susan and found links to several of her sex work-related publications, which provoked great interest among the group. The woman sitting with the laptop read the description of her book on topless dancers out loud, commenting on how she had used the women's own words and life histories to understand sex work as a form of feminized labor.

One of the residents, a former street sex worker whose main priority at the time was her addiction recovery, told Susan, "That's cool that you had them tell their story in their way" and then, using her characteristic sense of humor to relay serious information, explained, "See, you did that book with the dancers, but prostitution is a whole different ballgame. And for women who've been homeless and in an addiction, that's a whole different ballgame. And then women who've been in prison, that's a whole different ballgame, too. So you're in a whole bunch of different ballgames at once." Other women in the room nodded seriously at her observation, which sparked a whole series of thoughts about the differences between specific forms of sex work.

Being able to critically engage with her previous research work on their own terms not only served as a rapport-builder in that Susan "made sense" to the women as a participant-observer presence in their lives, but also made them more willing to educate her about the realities that shaped their worlds. A somewhat heated debate ensued following their discussion of the book, with a few women (predominantly street-based workers) arguing that there was no real difference between prostitution and topless dancing or, for that matter, between prostitution and being a stay-at-home mother dependent on a husband. One of the speakers held her ground, though, insisting that the higher visibility of street-based workers put them at infinitely higher risks of violence, arrest, and other forms of abuse, and approximately half the room agreed with her. Seeing the women split into camps in this way around her work prompted Susan to critically challenge some of her own ideas about sex work that, in turn, strengthened her ability to see nuances inherent in the project itself that she failed to notice previously.

Even when researchers have not carried out their work in a collaborative or participatory fashion, they can still endeavor to make their work available in more inclusive formats that include academics, sex workers, and harm reduction practitioners on equal terms. One potential means for researchers to engage in this work is through the production of a best practices document to share with other local organizations and social service providers who also engage with sex workers in some capacity. Such documents are concise and written in simple, straightforward language in order to reach the broadest audience possible, and some of the best examples have been produced by sex workers' rights organization.

Stella, a Montreal-based sex workers' rights organization, produced a thorough but brief one page leaflet entitled "Sex Workers and Research Ethics" that detailed the rights and responsibilities involved in conducting or participating in research (Stella 2006). The Chicago branch of the Sex Workers' Outreach Project (SWOP) produced a simple 12-point list called "How to Be an Ally to Sex Workers" (SWOP, n.d.), which they posted on their website. More academic examples of best practices guides for research with sex workers can be found in Overs and Longo (1996), and Allman and Ditmore (2009, 2011).

As projects evolve and develop, there inevitably will be space and time for assessment of the results and possible ways forward, and this can also be participatory. SWOP-Las Vegas' co-director feels that a research team of academics and sex workers could evaluate the success of their project in a number of ways. Participants and community members should be able to read or learn about the results of the study and feel that they were accurately portrayed, and ideally the work should inform policy in ways that improves sex workers' lives on their own terms. Additional potential benefits to be assessed include whether the study's results leads to greater empathy and cultural understanding, and if research participants benefitted as much as the researcher from the project.

SWOP-NOLA's director also recommends that the success of the project be measured in part by the amount of access provided to it upon its completion. In an ideal situation, participants would have a chance to meet and review the final product in order to catch any inaccuracies or problematic elements before publication. This assumes that all members are not only functionally literate, but literate at the level necessary in order to read and comprehend academic work in a specialized field. This is not likely to be the case in New Orleans, where 18 % of the population was functionally illiterate as of 2003 (National Center for Education Statistics 2003). Given these difficulties and the likelihood that they will be compounded by time constraints and other practicalities involved in academic publication, a question-and-answer session may be ideal to disseminate the findings, followed by a discussion in which group members can raise concerns about the content of the final product.

In conclusion, SWOP-NOLA's director stresses the importance of attempting to establish and maintain high levels of trust throughout the project, as there is an inevitable and obvious power imbalance in favor of the academic researchers directing the study. Ethical academic researchers will prioritize the concerns of sex workers in designing and carrying out participatory research, and, in doing so, the final product will respectfully treat the choices, experiences, and identities of those sex workers who have taken on considerable risk in order to work with them.

Conclusion

Susan Dewey

This book opened with two ethnographic anecdotes, both of which featured an anthropologist forced to confront her own motivations, decisions, and perspectives at particularly challenging moments in her research on sex work. In the preceding chapters, which are the product of Tiantian Zheng's and my combined total of 25 years of research engagement with sex workers, we sought to untangle some of the ethical dilemmas that sex work researchers face as well as to offer some possibilities for addressing these issues in research.

Findings and analysis presented in this book have detailed the divisive, potentially invasive, and, above all, complex politics of engaging in research with sex workers. We presented the potentially dangerous consequences of such research, including the possibility of perpetuating stereotypes that may, in turn, negatively influence legal or public policy in ways that cause further harm to sex workers. Likewise, we described difficulties inherent in trust- and rapport-building with individuals who have had a consistent experience of marginalization by those in positions of power, and the related difficulties in obtaining self-reported data on sexual or other health-related practices.

In our detailed accounts of successfully completed research on sex work, we reviewed the significant variations in how individuals uniquely understand and emotionally process their experiences of sex work. We also acknowledged that, for some sex workers, participation in research may present emotional difficulties or the potential for interpersonal or workplace discord. Chapters in this book featured discussions of the full continuum of sex work-related behaviors and practices, as well as the ethical concerns associated with each. For instance, those carrying out research with street-based or survival sex workers must additionally consider the ethics of engaging in remuneration that may prove coercive, or the difficulties inherent in maintaining contact with a transient population.

Our consideration of ethical issues in sex work research also contemplated gaps in the academic literature that might prove fruitful ground for further investigation. We devoted an entire chapter to participatory research with sex workers, which constitutes a relatively unexplored area of research design and offers the potential of collaborative work that may result in benefits to participants. Participatory sex work research projects that have been successfully carried out have relied upon sex workers' activist or harm reduction groups, and one interesting possibility for subsequent projects might lie in making a participatory project entirely sex worker-based, without the assistance of such groups.

From the formulation of research questions to the dissemination of findings, previous chapters have demonstrated that ethics must remain a central concern at all stages of the research process. Research questions must engage with the normative frameworks sex workers employ in their own lives, as well as the issues of concern to them. We encourage researchers to think about the research data they collect on such sensitive subject matter as a kind of gift that requires utmost assurance of reciprocity in the form of confidentiality protection. Everyone the researcher speaks to should receive the same protection and assurances, regardless of the affinities and bonds that the researcher might develop with particular individuals during fieldwork.

Researchers have a unique role in the stigmatized and often criminalized environment surrounding sex work, and this can seriously complicate their role between different individuals are parties who evince interest in sex work as a social issue. Although research participants may disclose information about illegal activities, researchers do not share law enforcements' sworn duty to uphold the law and incriminate those who violate it. Researchers similarly do not have the responsibility to intervene in individuals' life practices, even when they may cause harm to themselves or others, as do social workers. Likewise, it is uncommon for a researcher to be actively engaged in sex work and its intimate engagement with clients as a source of income generation. This completely unique, separate identity that researchers enjoy comes with a responsibility to report respondents' words and lives on their own terms while protecting the sources of this information.

Participants in research must be able to provide informed consent via the researcher's full disclosure of the research, its purposes, and the uses to which it will be put. Obtaining sex workers' verbal consent, rather than a signature on an official-looking form, serves two related functions by reducing risks to participants by eliminating any paper link between real identities and pseudonyms, and by reducing the risk that participants suspect that the researcher is a state agent of some kind. Researchers engaging in research in more organized sex work settings where informing clients might pose a risk of client loss to the business owner or to individual sex workers should endeavor to clarify distinctions between private locations where consent must be sought, and public venues where none is required.

Boundaries surrounding informed consent must continually face scrutiny and redefinition as relationships between the researcher and research participants change over time. This is particularly true as researchers begin to prepare material for publication and may feel the need to discuss the content and portrayal of the community with research participants. Researchers may find, for instance, that the bonds of friendship formed in the course of ethnographic fieldwork may not always make it easy for anyone to distinguish between when an individual is relaying information as a research participant and when she (or he) is communicating something as a friend and confidante. Researchers must consider this carefully as they prepare materials for publication.

The intimate connection between methodology and theory means that researchers must endeavor to respect the validity of sex workers' statements and experiences. Ideological preconceptions informing the research inevitably shape methodological strategies, and arguments presented throughout this book strongly favor actively incorporating sex workers in analyzing and interpreting their own worlds. In this way, researchers can work toward ensuring that their data and analysis accurately reflect the life realities of those who participated in their research.

Sex work research, as is the case in research with other marginalized and stigmatized populations, requires special attention in order to ensure that the research design incorporates the full spectrum of the diverse venues in which sex work takes place. This means that researchers should take special care to ensure that their research sample does not over-represent those sex workers who are the most easily accessible via streets, shelter, jail, or related venues. One solution to this quandary can be found in the practice of targeted sampling, developed by Watters and Biernacki (1988) in their work with injection drug users.

Targeted sampling involves initial spatial mapping of a community with high concentrations of the behavior under study, followed by ethnographic mapping of the social networks within these communities, then determining times and locations from which to draw the representative sample. Researchers should endeavor to demonstrate the diversity between different forms of sex work as well as diversity within each particular form including acute attention to class, ethno-racial identity and other factors that comprise personhood for individual sex workers.

Such responsible research in an ideologically charged environment can be complicated. Chapter 3 discussed the three prevailing and perhaps irreconcilable views on sex work, including abolitionist activists that view all sex work as a form of violence against women, sexual liberationists who see sex work as potentially empowering choice for women, and researchers who view these two extremes as opposite ends of a continuum experienced very differently by individuals. Although these debates have been ongoing since the inception of the broader questions raised by feminist activists in the 1970s, these issues have become even more polarized due to the injection of security discourse in the past decade.

Government positioning trafficking as a national security issue has only worsened conditions for many sex workers, who become distinguished into "innocent victims" (of trafficking) and "guilty whores" who choose sex work out of some misguided personal failure warranting state intervention through arrest and rehabilitation. The results, including raids on brothels in the name of rescuing women who may not desire this course of action, increased arrests and deportations, and the discourse of "modern-day slavery" discourse all reinforce the power of the state to legislate and intervene in what it regards as inappropriate or immoral sexual behavior.

Such prevailing beliefs can influence a researcher's likelihood of obtaining IRB approval, as cultural beliefs and stereotypes about sex work as deviant, dangerous, and criminal present difficulties for Board members encountering this type of research for the first time. In their proposals, researchers should endeavor to carefully detail other researchers' strategies for protecting participants by way of demonstrating their preparation to engage in new and pioneering research on what is becoming an increasingly well-trodden path.

In obtaining access to sex worker population, researchers typically form a relationship with a third party to help them gain this access, whether through an establishment such as a brothel or strip club, or through outreach projects or shelters. In doing so, the researcher must be careful to make her (or his) status as a researcher clear at all times, so as to avoid undue influence by others' political agendas or (in the case of police or other state agents/non-state groups) professional responsibilities. Women researchers need to additionally determine how they will respond to sexual overtures from potential clients. Indeed, women researchers should expect to interrogate their own uniquely embodied subjectivity throughout the course of their investigations into sex work.

Reciprocity and reflexivity are two important tools that help to ensure a sex worker-driven perspective. Forming bonds of friendship, assistance, and sharing personal information are all ways that researchers can become more embedded in the field. This, of course, comes with the caveat that one must remain keenly attuned to the nature of the field site and what information might be appropriately revealed there. In doing so, researchers should also reflect upon how they are processing the information they have collected, such as how their individual positionality shapes their interpretations or experiences of interacting with research participants.

Participatory research is one rather underexplored option in sex work research, as it places elements of the research design, implementation, and analysis process either partly or exclusively in the hands of individuals who engage in behaviors or practices that the research seeks to understand. Such research is complicated by the reality that many sex workers live/work in a criminalized or stigmatized environment that may inhibit their desire to participate in research due to the risks of arrest through exposure. Hence this chapter discussed ways of tackling resistance with advocacy/harm reduction groups, including reciprocity, spending time becoming a known and engaging figure embedded in the field.

As with any form of research design, participatory researchers must carefully question their own assumptions about organizations and their accompanying ideological stances, and accept that their own previously held notions about sex work may change as the research progresses. The great beauty of participatory research is that it allows points of view to evolve among all concerned as the project progresses from research design to analysis of the results. Participatory research can help to overcome some of the tensions inherent in research by carrying out research on behalf of a community, and in the case of sex workers this can be confined to a particular type of sex work, to sex workers in a certain geographical area or a sex worker demographic served by an organization. Once the community (and its boundaries) has been established, a series of meetings with community members determine the research's focus and central framing questions, although projects can vary in the degree of participation involved. Once participatory work is completed, researchers work with the community to decide how to disseminate their findings in meaningful ways.

Ethnographic examples presented throughout this book firmly underscore that individuals experience sex work in ways that are as many and varied as the individuals themselves. Some sex workers envision their labor as an emancipatory calling, others see it as a way to negotiate economic hardship, and still others experience sex work as demeaning and harmful. The work of anthropologists in telling their stories, on sex workers' own terms, remains a deeply political act in which research findings do not always correspond with state law or policy and may even indicate the need for significant social and political change. In this and in myriad other ways documented throughout this book, engaging in sex work research involves courage, fortitude, and, above all, a willingness to speak the truth to power.

Erratum to: Ethical Research with Sex Workers

Susan Dewey and Tiantian Zheng

Erratum to:
S. Dewey and T. Zheng, *Ethical Research with Sex Workers*, SpringerBriefs in Anthropology, DOI 10.1007/978-1-4614-6492-1

In the Foreword, the reference list is missing. Please find the reference list below.

References

Chacon, Richard, and Ruben Mendoza. 2012a. Introduction. In *The ethics of anthropology and Amerindian research: reporting on environmental degradation and warfare*, eds. R. Chacon, and R. Mendoza, 1–26. New York: Springer.

Chacon, Richard, and Ruben Mendoza. 2012b. Discussion and conclusions. In *The ethics of anthropology and Amerindian research: reporting on environmental degradation and warfare*, eds. R. Chacon, and R. Mendoza, 451–503. New York: Springer.

Gregor, Thomas, and Daniel Gross. 2004. "Guilt by association: the culture of accusation and the American anthropological association's investigation of darkness in El Dorado." *American Anthropologist* 106(4):687–698.

The online version of the original chapter can be found under DOI 10.1007/978-1-4614-6492-1

S. Dewey and T. Zheng, *Ethical Research with Sex Workers*,   E1
SpringerBriefs in Anthropology and Ethics,
DOI: 10.1007/978-1-4614-6492-1_5, © The Author(s) 2013

Works Cited

Abrams, Laura S. 2000. Guardians of virtue: The social reformers and the 'girl problem', 1890–1920. *Social Service Review* 74: 436–452.

Addams, Jane. 1912. *A new conscience and an ancient evil*. New York: Macmillan.

Adelman, Clem. 1992. Kurt lewin and the origins of action research. *Educational Action Research* 1(1): 7–24.

Agustín, Laura María. 2005. New research directions: The cultural study of commercial sex. *Sexualities* 8(5): 618–631.

Agustín, Laura María. 2004. Alternate ethics, or: Telling lies to researchers. *Research For Sex Work* 2004: 6–7.

Alexander, Priscilla. 1997. Feminism, Sex Workers And Human Rights. In *Whores And Other Feminists*, ed. Jill Nagle, 83–97. New York: Routledge.

Allen, Jafari Sinclaire. 2007. Means of desire's production: Male sex labor in Cuba. *Identities: Global Studies in Culture and Power* 14(1/2): 183–202.

Allison, Anne. 1994. *Nightwork: Sexuality, pleasure and corporate masculinity in a Tokyo hostess club*. Chicago: University of Chicago Press.

Allman, Dan and Melissa Ditmore. 2009. Good practice for sex workers' participation in biomedical HIV prevention trials. GPP programmatic report for the AIDS Vaccine Advocacy Coalition (AVAC). *Research For Sex Work (R4SW 7): Sex Workers' Health, HIV/AIDS, Ethical Issues Care & Research* 7: 3–5.

Almodovar, Norma Jean. 1993. *Cop to call girl: Why i quit the LAPD to make an honest living as a Beverly Hills prostitute*. New York: Simon & Schuster.

American Anthropological Association. 1998. Code of Ethics. Accessed from: http://www.aaanet.org/committees/ethics/ethcode.htm.

Barry, Kathleen. 1979. *Female sexual slavery*. Englewood Cliffs: Prentice Hall.

Barton, Bernadette. 2006. *Stripped: Inside the lives of exotic dancers*. New York: New York University Press.

Behar, Ruth. 1996. Introduction: Out of exile. In *Women writing culture*, eds. Ruth Behar and Deborah A. Gordon, 1–32. Berkeley: University of California Press.

Belle de Jour. 2010. *Belle's best bits: A london call girl reveals her favorite adventures*. London: Orion Publishing.

Belle de Jour. 2009. *Belle de Jour's guide to men*. London: Orion.

Belle de Jour. 2008. *Secret Diary of a Call Girl*. New York: Grand Central Publishing.

Belle de Jour. 2006. *Belle de Jour: Diary of an unlikely Call Girl*.

Bellér-Hann, Ildiko. 1995. Prostitution and its effects in Northeast Turkey. *European Journal of Women's Studies* 2: 219–235.

Bennachie, Calum. (2010). Comment On Farley's 'What *Really* Happened in New Zealand in New Zealand After Prostitution Was Decriminalized in 2003? Accessed from:

http://independent.academia.edu/CalumBennachie/Papers/1086657/Comment_on_
Melissa_Farleys_claims_regarding_decriminalisation_of_sex_work_in_New_Zealand.

Benoit, Cecilia, and Alison Millar. 2001 *Dispelling myths and understanding realities: Working conditions, health status, and exiting experiences of sex workers.* Victoria: Prostitutes, Education, Empowerment, and Resource Society.

Bernstein, Elizabeth. 2005. Desire, demand, and the commerce of sex. In *Regulating Sex: The politics of intimacy and identity,* ed. Elizabeth Bernstein, and Laurie Schaffner, 101–125. New York: Routledge.

Berrett, Dan. 2011. Anthropologists grapple with drawing the line between research and advocacy. *The Chronicle of Higher Education* 58(15).

Bhutta, Zulfiqar A. 2004. Beyond informed consent. *Bulletin of the World Health Organization* 82(10): 771–777.

Bindman, Jo. 1998. An international perspective on slavery in the sex industry. In *Global sex workers: Rights, rescue, and redefinition,* ed. Kamala Kempadoo, and Jo Doezema, 65–68. New York: Routledge.

Bourgois, Philip. 1995. *In search of respect: Selling crack in El Barrio.* Cambridge: Cambridge University Press.

Bourgois, Philippe, Bridget Prince, and Andrew Moss. 2004. The everyday violence of Hepatitis C among young women who inject drugs in San Francisco. *Human Organization* 63(3): 253–264.

Bowman, Glenn. 1989. Fucking tourists: Sexual relations and tourism in Jerusalem's old city. *Critique of Anthropology* 9(2): 77–93.

Boyton, Petra. 2002. Life on the streets: The experiences of community researchers in a study of prostitution. *Journal of Community and Applied Social Psychology* 12(1): 1–12.

Bradley, Mindy. 2007. Girlfriends, wives, and strippers: Managing stigma in exotic dancer relationships. *Deviant Behavior* 28: 379–406.

Brennan, Denise. 2004. *What's love got to do with it? Transnational desires and sex tourism in the Dominican Republic.* Durham, NC: Duke University Press.

Brents, Barbara, Crystal Jackson, and Kathryn Hausbeck. 2009. *The state of sex: Tourism, sex and sin in the New American Heartland.* New York: Routledge.

Brewer, Devon, Jonathan Dudek, John Potterat, Stephen Muth, John Roberts, and Donald Woodhouse. 2006. Extent, trends, and perpetrators of prostitution-related homicide in the United States. *Journal of Forensic Science* 51: 1101–1108.

Brewis, Joanna. 2005. Signing my life away? Researching sex and organization. *Organization* 12(4): 493–510.

Brody, Stuart, John Potterat, Stephen Muth, and Donald Woodhouse. 2005. Psychiatric and characterological factors relevant to excessive mortality in a long-term cohort of prostitute women. *Journal of Sex and Marital Therapy* 31: 97–112.

Brooks, Margaret and Donna Hughes. 2009. International Sex Radicals Campaign To Keep Prostitution Decriminalized in Rhode Island. Accesssd from: http://www.citizensagainsttraffic king.com/uploads/Sex_Radicals_Target_Rhode Island.pdf.

Browne, Jan, and Victor Minichiello. 1996. The social and work context of commercial sex between men: A research note. *Australian and New Zealand Journal of Sociology* 32(1): 86–92.

Bruckert, Chris. 2002. *Taking It Off, Putting It On: Women in the strip trade.* London: The Women's Press.

Buchanan, David. 2009. Ethical dilemmas in conducting field research with injection drug users. In *Research with high risk populations: Building science, ethics, and law,* eds. David Buchanan, Celia Fisher, and Lance Gable, 149–65. Washington, DC: American Psychological Association.

Cabezas, Amalia. 2009. *Economies of desire: Sex and tourism in the Dominican Republic.* Durham, NC: Duke University Press.

Campbell, Rosie. 2001. 'We shouldn't have to put up with this': Street sex work and violence. *Criminal Justice Matters* 42: 12–13.

Capous-Desyllas, Moshoula. 2011. Photovoice with sex workers for community awareness, empowerment and resistance. In *Creative arts in research for community and cultural change,* ed. Cheryl McLean, and Robert Kelly, 363–384. Calgary: Detselig Temeron Press.

Capous-Desyllas, Moshoula. 2010. *Visions and voices: An arts-based qualitative study using Photovoice to understand the needs and aspirations of diverse women working in the sex industry.* PhD diss., Portland State University.

Caputo, Gail. 2008. *Out in the storm: Drug-addicted women living as shoplifters and sex workers.* Boston: Northeastern University Press.

CDC/Centers for Disease Control and Prevention. 2010. The National Intimate Partner and Sexual Violence Survey. Accessed from: http://www.cdc.gov/violenceprevention/nisvs/.

Chang, Sung. 2011. Prostitutes + condoms = AIDS?: The Leadership Act, USAID, and the HHS guidelines' failures to define 'promoting prostitution'. *The American University Journal of Gender, Social Policy, and the Law* 19(1): 373–399.

Chapkis, Wendy. 1997. *Live Sex Acts: Women performing erotic labor.* New York: Routledge.

Chapkis, Wendy. 2000. Power and control in the commercial sex trade. In *Sex for sale: Prostitution, pornography, and the sex industry,* ed. Ronald Weizer, 181–201. New York: Routledge.

Church, Stephanie, Marion Henderson, Marina Barnard, and Graham Hart. 2001. Violence by clients towards female prostitutes in different work settings: Questionnaire survey. *British Medical Journal* 322: 524–525.

Clements-Nolle, Kristen, and Ari Bachrach. 2003. Community based participatory research with a hidden population: The transgender community health project. In *Community based participatory research for health,* ed. Meredith Minkler, and Nina Wallerstein, 332–343. San Francisco: Jossey-Bass.

Coffey, Amanda. 1999. *The ethnographic self: Fieldwork and the representation of identity.* London: Sage.

Cole, Susan. 1987. Sexual politics: Contradictions and explosions. In *Good Girls/Bad Girls,* ed. Laurie Bell, 33–36. Seattle, WA: Seal Press.

Corbin, Juliet, and Janice M. Morse. 2003. The unstructured interactive interview: Issues of reciprocity and risks when dealing with sensitive topics. *Qualitative Inquiry* 9(3): 335–354.

Cowburn, Malcolm. 2005. Confidentiality and public protection: Ethical dilemmas in qualitative research with adult male sex offenders. *Journal of Sexual Aggression: An International, Interdisciplinary Forum For Research, Theory And Practice* 11(1): 49–63.

Crago, Anna-Louise. 2008. *Our lives matter: Sex workers unite for health and rights.* New York: Open Society Institute.

Crewswell, John W. 2008. *Qualitative Inquiry and Research Design: Choosing among five approaches.* Thousand Oaks, CA: Sage.

Cwikel, Julie, and Elizabeth Hoban. 2005. Contentious issues in research on trafficked women working in the sex industry: Study design, ethics, and methodology. *Journal of Sex Research* 42(4): 306–316.

Dalla, Rochelle. 2001. Et Tú Brutè?: A qualitative analysis of streetwalking prostitutes' interpersonal support networks. *Journal of Family Issues* 22: 1066–1085.

Dalla, Rochelle. 2003. When the bough breaks: Examining intergenerational parent-child relationship patterns among street-level sex workers and their parents and children. *Applied Developmental Science* 7(4): 216–228.

Dalla, Rochelle, Yan Xia, and Heather Kennedy. 2003. 'You just give them what they want and pray they don't kill you': Street-level sex workers' reports of victimization, personal resources and coping strategies. *Violence Against Women* 9(11): 1367–1394.

Damianakis, Thecla, and Michael R. Woodford. 2012. Qualitative research with small connected communities: Generating new knowledge while upholding research ethics. *Qualitative Health Research* 22(5): 708–718.

Day, Sophie. 2007. *On the game: Women and sex work.* London: Pluto.

Day, Sophie, and Helen Ward (eds.). 2004. *Sex Work, Mobility And Health In Europe.* London: Kegan Paul.

Day, Sophie, and Helen Ward. 2001. Violence towards female prostitutes. *British Medical Journal* 323: 230.

Delacoste, Frederique, and Priscilla Alexander (eds.). 1987. *Sex work: Writings by women in the sex industry.* San Francisco: Cleis.

Deshotels, Tina, and Craig J. Forsyth. 2006. Strategic flirting and the emotional tab of exotic dancing. *Deviant Behavior* 27: 223–241.

Dewey, Susan. 2008. *Hollow bodies: Institutional responses to sex trafficking in Armenia, Bosnia and India*. Sterling, VA: Kumarian Press.

Dewey, Susan. 2011. *Neon wasteland: On love, motherhood, and sex work in a Rust Belt Town*. Berkeley: University of California Press.

Dewey, Susan. 2012. The feminized labor of sex work: Two decades of feminist historical and ethnographic research. *Labor: Studies in Working-Class History of the Americas* 9(2): 113–132.

Dewey, Susan, and Patty Kelly (eds.). 2011. *Policing pleasure: Sex work, policy, and the state in global perspective*. New York: New York University Press.

Dewey, Susan (ed.). 2011. Special issue: Demystifying sex work and sex workers. *Wagadu, a Journal of Transnational Women's and Gender Studies* 8:1–242.

Dines, Gail. 2012. A feminist response to Weitzer. *Violence Against Women* 18(4): 512–517.

Ditmore, Melissa and Dan Allman. 2011. Who is Helsinki? Sex workers advise improving communication for good participatory practice in clinical trials. *Health Education Research*. Accessed from: http://her.oxfordjournals.org/content/early/2011/01/24/her.cyq087.full.

Ditmore, Melissa Hope, Antonia Levy, and Alys Willman (eds.). 2010. *Sex work matters: Exploring money, power and intimacy in the sex industry*. London: Zed Books.

Doezema, Jo. 2000. Loose women or lost women?: The re-emergence of the myth of white slavery in contemporary discourses of trafficking in women. *Gender Issues* 18(1): 23–50.

Doezema, Jo. 1998. Forced to choose: Beyond the voluntary vs. forced prostitution dichotomy. In *Global sex workers: Rights, resistance, and redefintion*, eds. Kamala Kempadoo and Jo Doezema, 34–50. New York: Routledge.

Dudash, Tawnya. 1997. Peepshow Feminism. In *Whores and other feminists*, ed. Jill Nagle, 98–118. New York: Routledge.

Dunlap, Eloise, Bruce Johnson and Doris Randolph. 2009. Ethical and legal dilemmas in ethnographic field research: Three case studies of distressed inner-city families. In *Research with high risk populations: building science, ethics, and law*, eds. David Buchanan, Celia Fisher, and Lance Gable, 207–229. Washington, DC: American Psychological Association.

Dworkin, Andrea. 1997. *Life and death: Unapologetic writings on the continuing war against women*. New York: The Free Press.

Dworkin, Andrea. 1993. Prostitution and male supremacy. Presentation "Prostitution: From Academia To Activism," sponsored by the Michigan Journal of Gender and Law delivered at the University of Michigan Law School, Ann Arbor

Dworkin, Andrea. 1981. *Pornography: Men possessing women*. London: The Women's Press.

Dworkin, Andrea. 1987. *Intercourse*. New York: Free Press.

Edwards, Jessica, Carolyn Halpern, and Wendee Wechsberg. 2006. Correlates of exchanging sex for drugs or money among women who use crack cocaine. *AIDS Education and Prevention* 18(5): 420–429.

Egan, Danielle. 2006. *Dancing for dollars and paying for love: Relationships between exotic dancers and their regulars*. New York: Palgrave MacMillan.

Egan, Danielle, Katherine Frank, and Merri Lisa Johnson, (eds.). *Flesh for fantasy: Producing and consuming exotic dance*. New York: Thunder's Mouth Press

El Bassel, Nabila, Susan Witte, Takeshi Wada, Louisa Gilbert, and Joyce Wallace. 2001. Correlates of partner violence among female street-based sex workers: Substance abuse, history of child abuse, and HIV risks. *AIDS Patient Care and STDs* 15: 41–51.

Erickson, David John, and Richard Tewksbury. 2000. The 'Gentlemen' in the club: A typology of strip club patrons. *Deviant Behavior* 21: 271–293.

Erickson, Patricia, Jennifer Butters, Patti McGillicuddy, and Ase Hallgren. 2000. Crack and prostitution: Gender, myths and experiences. *Journal of Drug Issues* 30: 767–788.

Etherington, Kim. 2007. Ethical research in reflexive relationships. *Qualitative Inquiry* 13(5): 599–616.

Farley, Melissa. 2007. *Prostitution and trafficking in Nevada: Making the connections*. San Francisco: Prostitution Research & Education.

Farley, Melissa. 1998. Prostitution, violence, and post-traumatic stress disorder. *Women and Health* 27(3): 37–49.

Farley, Melissa. 2004. Bad for the body, bad for the heart: Prostitution harms women even if legalized or decriminalized. *Violence Against Women* 10: 1087–1125.

Ferrell, Jeff, and Mark S. Hamm. 1998. *Ethnography at the edge: Crime, deviance, and field research*. Boston: Northeastern University Press.

Fisher, Celia, Matthew Oransky, Meena Mahadevan, Merrill Singer, Greg Mirhej, and Derrick G. Hodge. 2009. Do drug abuse researchers have a duty to protect third parties from HIV Transmission? moral perspectives of street drug users. In *Research with high risk populations: Building science, ethics, and law*, eds. David Buchanan, Celia Fisher, and Lance Gable, 189–206. Washington, DC: American Psychological Association.

Ford, Katie. 1998. Evaluating prostitution as a human service occupation. In *Prostitution: On whores, hustlers, and johns*, ed. James Elias, Vern L. Bullough, Veronica Elias, and Gwen Brewer, 420–434. Amherst, NY: Prometheus.

Frank, Katherine. 2002. *G-strings and sympathy: Strip club regulars and male desire*. Durham, NC: Duke University Press.

Frank, Katherine. 2007. Thinking critically about strip club research. *Sexualities* 10(4): 501–517.

French, D. 1998. *Working: My life as a prostitute*. New York: Pinnacle Books.

Frembgen, Jurgen. 2008. Marginality, sexuality and the body: Professional masseurs in Urban Muslim Punjab. *Asia Pacific Journal of Anthropology* 9(1): 1–28.

Golder, Seana, and T.K. Logan. 2007. Correlates and predictors of women's sex trading over time among a sample of out-of-treatment drug abusers. *AIDS and Behavior* 11(2007): 628–640.

Goldman, Abigail. 2008. Bewildered academics pore over sex-trade Hysteria: They try to figure out how they got steamrolled. *Las Vegas Sun*. www.lasvegassun.com/news/2008/jan/31/bewildered-academics-pore-over-sex-trade-hysteria. Accessed from 31 Jan 2008.

Goodman, Robert. 2001. Community-based participatory research: questions and challenges to an essential approach. *Journal of Public Health Management Practice* 7(5): 5–7.

Gordon, Avery. 1997. *Ghostly matters: Haunting and the sociological imagination*. Minneapolis: University of Minnesota Press.

Guillemin, Marilys, and Lynn Gillam. 2004. Ethics, reflexivity and ethically important moments in research. *Qualitative Inquiry* 10(2): 261–280.

Hann, Chris, and Ildiko Bellér-Hann. 1992. Samovars and sex on Turkey's Russian markets. *Anthropology Today* 8(4): 3–6.

Hanna, Judith Lynne. 2012. *Naked truth: Strip clubs, Democracy, and a Christian right*. Austin: University of Texas Press.

Hanna, Judith Lynne. 1998. Undressing the first amendment and corseting the striptease dancer. *The Drama Review* 42(2): 38–69.

Hart, Angie. 1998. *Buying and selling power: Anthropological reflections on prostitution in Spain*. Oxford: Westview Press.

Hastings, Donnan, and Fiona Magowan. 2010. *The anthropology of sex*. Oxford: Berg.

Hearn, Jeff. 1998. *The violence of men*. London: Sage.

Hearn, Jeff, Phil Raws, Roger Barford, Robbie Dacres, and David Riley. 1993. Working guidelines: Men interviewing men. In *Researching men and researching men's violence*, ed. Jeff Hearn, 33–53. Research Unit on violence, abuse and gender relations. Bradford: University of Bradford.

Henry, Ray. 2009. Academic oppose Rhode Island banning indoor prostitution. http://www2.turnto10.com/news/2009/aug/03/academics_oppose_ri_banning_indoor_prostitution-ar-52342/. Accessed from 3 Aug 2009.

Hoang, Kimberly Kay. 2011. 'She's not a low-class dirty girl!': Sex work in Ho Chi Minh City, Vietnam. *Contemporary Ethnology* 40(4): 367–396.

Hubbard, Phil. 1999. Researching female sex work: Reflections on geographical exclusion, critical methodologies and 'useful' knowledge. *Area* 31(3): 229–237.

Hughes, Donna. 2003. The world's sex slaves need liberation, not condoms. *The Weekly Standard* 8(23).

Hughes, Donna. 2000. Men create the demand; Women are the supply: lecture on sexual exploitation, lecture at Queen Sofia Center, Valencia, Spain. www.uri.edu/artsci/wms/hughes/demand.htm. Accessed from Nov 2000.

Inciardi, James, and Hilary Surratt. 2000. Drug use, street crime and sex trading among cocaine-dependent women: Implications for public health and criminal justice policy. *Journal of Psychoactive Drugs* 33: 378–389.

Israel, B. 2003. Schulz A, Parker E, Becker A, Allen A, Guzman J R. Critical issues in developing and following community base participatory research principles. In *Community Based Participatory Research for Health*, ed. Meredith Minkler, Nina Wallerstein, 53–76. San Francisco: Jossey-Bass.

Izugbara, Chimaraoke. 2010. Client retention and health among sex workers in Nairobi, Kenya. *Archives of Sexual Behavior* 41(3): 21–29.

Izugbara, Chimaraoke. 2007. Constituting the unsafe: Nigerian sex workers' notions of unsafe sexual conduct. *African Studies Review* 50(3): 29–49.

Jackson, Lois, Alexandra Highcrest, and Randall A. Coates. 1992. Varied potential risks of HIV infection among prostitutes. *Social Science and Medicine* 35(3): 281–286.

Jascia-Lees, Frances, Patricia Sharp, and Colleen Ballerino Cohen. 1989. The postmodernist turn in anthopology: Cautions from a feminist perspective. *Signs* 15(1): 7–33.

Jennes, Valerie. 1990. From sex as sin to sex as work. *Social Problems* 37(3): 403–420.

Katsulis, Yasmina. 2008. *Sex work and the city: The social geography of health and safety in Tijuana, Mexico*. Austin: University of Texas Press.

Kaiser, Karen. 2009. Protecting respondent confidentiality in qualitative research. *Qualitative Health Research* 19: 1632–1641.

Kelly, Patty. 2008. *Lydia's open door: Inside Mexico's most modern brothel*. Berkeley: University of California Press.

Kempadoo, Kamala, and Jo Doezeman (eds.). 1998. *Global sex workers: Rights resistance and redefinitions*. New York: Routledge.

Kulick, Don. 1998. *Travesti: Sex, gender and culture among Brazilian transgendered prostitutes*. Chicago: University of Chicago Press.

Kunzel, Regina G. 1993. *Fallen women, problem girls: Unmarried mothers and the professionalization of social work 1890–1945*. New Haven: Yale University Press.

Lee, Raymond M. 1990. *Doing research on sensitive topics*. London: Sage.

Lee, Raymond M, and Claire M. Renzetti. 1990. The problems of researching sensitive topics: An overview and introduction. *American Behavioral Scientist* 33: 510–528.

Leigh, Carol. 1998. The continuing saga of Scarlot Harlot III. In *Sex work: Writings by women in the sex industry*, ed. Frederique Delacoste, and Patricia Alexander, 59–61. San Franciso: Cleis Press.

Lerum, Kari. 1999. Twelve-step feminism makes sex workers sick: How the state the recovery movement turn radical women into 'Useless Citizens'. In *Sex work and sex workers*, eds. Barry Michael Dank, and Roberto Refinetti, 7–36. Brunswick: Transaction Books.

Lever, Janet, and David E. Kanouse. 1998. Using qualitative methods to study the hidden world of offstreet prostitution in Los Angeles County. In *Prostitution: On whores, hustlers, and Johns*, ed. James Elias, Vern L. Bullough, Veronica Elias, and Gwen Brewer, 396–406. Amherst: Prometheus.

Lewis, Jacqueline. 2000. Controlling lap dancing: Law, morality and sex work. In *Sex for sale*, ed. Ronald Weitzer, 203–216. New York: Routledge.

Lewis, Jacqueline. 2006. I'll scratch your back if you'll scratch mine: the role of reciprocity, power, and autonomy in the strip club. *The Canadian Review of Sociology and Anthropology* 43(3): 297–311.

Leyla, Keough. 2010. Driven women: Reconceptualizing the traffic in women in the margins of Europe through the case of Gagauz mobile domestics in Istanbul. *Anthropology of East*

Europe Review 21. Accessed from: http://scholarworks.iu.edu/journals/index.php/aeer/article/view/347/422.

Limon, Joes E. 1994. *Dancing with the devil: Society and cultural poetics in Mexican-American South Texas*. Madison: University of Wisconsin Press.

Lumby, Catharine, Kath Albury, and Alan McKee. 2008. *The porn report*. Melbourne: Melbourne University Publishing.

MacKinnon, Catharine A. 1989. *Toward a feminist theory of the state*. Cambridge: Harvard University Press.

MacKinnon, Catharine A. 1987. *Feminism unmodified: Discourses on law and life*. Cambridge: Harvard University Press.

Magnanti, Brooke. 2012. *The sex myth: Why everything we're told is wrong*. London: George Weidenfeld &Nicholson.

Maher, Lisa, and Richard Curtis. 1992. Women on the edge of crime: Crack Cocaine and the changing contexts of street-level sex work in New York City. *Crime, Law, and Social Change* 18: 221–258.

Manderson, Lenore. 1992. Public sex performances in Patpong: Explorations of the edges of imagination. *Journal of Sex Research* 29(4): 451–475.

Mattley, Christine. 1997. Field research with phone sex workers. In *Researching sexual violence against women*, ed. Martin Schwartz, 146–158. London: Sage.

McClelland, Gabrielle, and Robert Newell. 2008. A qualitative study of the experiences of mothers involved in street-based prostitution and problematic substance use. *Journal of Research in Nursing* 13: 437–447.

McLeod, Eileen. 1982. *Working women: Prostitution now*. London: Cromm.

Melrose, Margaret. 2002. Labor pains: Some considerations on the difficulties of researching juvenile prostitution. *International Journal of Social Research Methodology* 5(4): 333–351.

Miller, Franklin G., and Alan Wertheimer. 2007. Facing up to paternalism in research ethics. *Hastings Centre Report* 37(3): 24–34.

Miller, Jody. 1993. Your life is on the line every night you're on the streets': Victimization and resistance among street prostitutes. *Humanity and Society* 17: 422–446.

Mitchell, Gregory. 2011. Turboconsumers™ in paradise: Tourism, civil rights, and Brazil's gay sex industry. *American Ethnologist* 38(4): 666–682.

Montgomery, Heather. 2001. *Modern Babylon? Prostituting children in Thailand*. Oxford: Berghahn.

Moodyson, Lukas. 2002. *Lilja 4-Ever*. Stockholm, Sweden: Film i Väst.

Moore, Henrietta. 1995. Master narratives: Anthropology and writing. In *A passion for difference*, 107–128. Bloomington: Indiana University Press.

Nadon, Susan, Catherine Koverol, and Eduard Schludermann. 1998. Antecedents to prostitution: Childhood victimization. *Journal of Interpersonal Violence* 13(2): 206–221.

National Center for Education Statistics. 2003. State & County estimates of low literacy: New Orleans. Accessed from: http://nces.ed.gov/naal/estimates/StateEstimates.aspx.

Nencel, Lorraine. 2001. *Ethnography and prostitution in Peru*. London: Pluto Press.

NIEHS/National Institute of Environmental Health Sciences. 2011. What is ethics in research and why is it important? Accessed from: http://www.niehs.nih.gov/research/resources/bioethics/whatis/.

NOPD/New Orleans Police Department. 2011. Media advisory: Press conference to discuss project HEAT, NOPD 2011. Accessed from: http://www.nola.gov/en/PRESS/New-Orleans-Police-Department/All-Articles/20110908-MEDIA-ADVISORY-Press-Conference-to-Discuss-Project-Heat.

Norton-Hawk, Maureen. 2004. A comparison of pimp- and non-pimp-controlled women. *Violence Against Women* 10: 189–194.

O'Doherty, Tamara. 2011. Victimization in off-street sex industry work. *Violence Against Women* 17(7): 944–963.

O'Neill, Maggie. 2007. Community safety, rights and recognition: Towards a coordinated prostitution strategy. *Community Safety Journal* 6(1): 45–52.

O'Neill, Maggie, Rosie Campbell, Phil Hubbard, Jane Pitcher, and Jane Scoular. 2008. Living with the other: Street sex work, contigent communities and degrees of tolerance. *Crime, Media Culture* 4: 73–93.

O'Neill, Maggie, and Rosie Campbell. 2006. Street sex work and local communities: Creating discursive spaces for genuine consultation and inclusion. In *Sex work now*, ed. Rosie Campbell, and Maggie O'Neill, 33–61. Cullompton: Willan.

Orchard, Treena. 2012. Sex work in the forest city: experiences of sex work beginnings, types, and clientele among women in London, Ontario. *Sexuality Research and Social Policy* 9: 350–362.

Padilla, Mark. 2007. *Caribbean pleasure industry: Tourism, sexuality, and aids in the Dominican Republic*. Chicago: University of Chicago Press.

Parker, Richard. 1999. *Beneath the equator: Cultures of desire, male homosexuality, and emerging gay communities in Brazil*. New York: Routledge.

Parsons, Jeffrey T. 2005. Researching the world's oldest profession: Introduction. *Journal of Psychology and Human Sexuality* 17(1–2): 1–3.

Perkins, Roberta, and Frances Lovejoy. 1996. Healthy and unhealthy lifestyles of female brothel workers and call girls (private sex workers) in Sydney. *Australian and New Zealand Journal of Public Health* 20(5): 512–516.

Pettiway, Leon. 1996. *Honey, honey, Miss Thang: Being black, Gay, and on the streets*. Philadelphia: Temple University Press.

Pettiway, Leon. 1997. *Workin' it: Women living through drugs and crime*. Philadelphia: Temple University Press.

Pons, Ignasi, and Victoria Serra. 1998. Female prostitution In Spain: Neither criminals nor victims. In *Prostitution: On whores, hustlers, and Johns*, ed. James Elias, Vern Bullough, Veronica Elias, and Gwen Brewer, 493–500. Amherst: Prometheus.

Porter, Judith, and Louis Bonilla. 2009. Drug use, HIV, and the ecology of street prostitution. In *Sex for sale*, ed. Ronald Weitzer, 163–186. New York: Routledge.

Potterat, John, Devon Brewer, Stephen Muth, Richard Rothenberg, Donald Woodhouse, John Muth, Heather Stites, and Stuart Brody. 2004. Mortality in a long-term open cohort of prostitute women. *American Journal of Epidemiology* 159(8): 778–785.

Pringle, Helen. 2011. The porn report: A studied indifference to harm. Australian Broadcasting Company (ABC) Religion and Ethics. Accessed from: http://www.abc.net.au/religion/articles/2011/09/06/3310775.htm.

Punch, Maurice. 1994. Politics and ethics in qualitative research. In *Handbook of qualitative research*, ed. Norman K. Denzin, and Yvonna S. Lincoln, 83–97. Thousand Oaks: Sage.

Pyett, Priscilla M. 1998. Researching with sex workers: A privilege and a challenge. In *Prostitution: on whores, hustlers, and Johns*, ed. James Elias, Vern Bullough. Veronica Elias, and Gwen Brewer, 368–375. Amherst: Prometheus.

Pyett, Priscilla M., and Deborah J. Warn. 1997. Vulnerability on the streets: Female sex workers and HIV risk. *AIDS Care* 9(5): 539–547.

Quinet, Kenna. 2011. Prostitutes as victims of serial homicide: Trends and case characteristics, 1970–2009. *Homicide Studies* 15: 74–100.

Raphael, Jody, and Deborah Shapiro. 2004. Violence in indoor and outdoor prostitution venues. *Violence Against Women* 10: 126–139.

Raymond, Janice. 2004. Ten reasons for not legalizing prostitution and a legal response to the demand for prostitution. In *Prostitution, trafficking and traumatic stress*, ed. Melissa Farley, 315–332. Binghamton: Haworth Press.

Rekart, Michael. 2005. Sex work harm reduction. *Lancet* 366: 2123–2134.

Reuben, Jacqueline, Chris Serio-Chapman, Christopher Welsh, Richard Matens, and Susan Sherman. 2011. Correlates of current transactional sex among a sample of female exotic dancers in Baltimore, MD. *Journal of Urban Health* 88(2): 342–351.

Roche, Brenda, Alan Neaigus, and Maureen Miller. 2005. Street smarts and urban myths: Women, sex work, and the role of storytelling in risk reduction and rationalization. *Medical Anthropology Quarterly* 19(2): 149–170.

Romero-Daza, Nancy. 2003. Nobody gives a damn if i live or die: Violence, drugs and street-level prostitution in inner city Hartford, Connecticut. *Medical Anthropology* 22(2003): 233–259.

Salfati, Gabrielle. 2009. Street prostitute homicide: An overview of the literature and a comparison to sexual and non-sexual female victim homicide. In *Safer sex in the city: The experience and management of street prostitution*, ed. David Canter, Maria Ioannou, and Donna Youngs, 51–81. Aldershot: Ashgate.

Salfati, Gabrielle, Allison James, and Lynn Ferguson. 2008. Prostitute homicides: A descriptive study. *Journal of Interpersonal Violence* 23: 505–543.

Sanders, Teela. 2004. A continuum of risk? Management of health, physical and emotional risks by female sex workers. *Sociology of Health and Illness* 26(4): 557–574.

Sanders, Teela. 2006. Sexing up the subject; methodological nuances in researching the female sex industry. *Sexualities* 9(4): 449–468.

Scheper-Hughes, Nancy. 2000. Ire in Ireland. *Ethnography* 1: 117–140.

Schmidt, Peter. 2011. Scholars of legal brothels offer a new take on the 'oldest' profession. *The Chronicle of Higher Education.* Accessed from: chronicle.com/article/Scholars-of-Legal-Brothels/129047.

Schilt, Kristen, and Laurel Westbrook. 2009. Doing gender, doing heteronormativity: 'Gender Normals', transgender people, and the social maintenance of heterosexuality. *Gender and Society* 23(4): 440–464.

Schweitzer, Dahlia. 2001. Striptease: the art of spectacle and transgression. *Journal of Popular Culture* 34(1): 65–75.

Scott, Julie. 1995. Sexual and national boundaries in tourism. *Annals of Tourism Research* 22(2): 385–403.

Seal, David Wyatt, Frederick R. Bloom, and Anton M. Somlai. 2000. Dilemmas in conducting qualitative sex research in applied field settings. *Health Education Behavior* 27(1): 10–23.

Shannon, Kate, Vicki Bright, Kate Gibson, and Mark Tyndall. 2007a. Sexual and drug-related vulnerabilities for HIV infection among women engaged in survival sex work in Vancouver, Canada. *Canadian Journal of Public Health* 98: 465–469.

Shannon, Kate, Vicki Bright, Allinott Shari, Alexon Debbie, Gibson Kata, and Tyndall Mark. 2007. Community-based HIV prevention research among substance-using women in survival sex work: The Maka Project Partnership. *Harm Reduction Journal* 4: 20–26.

Shaver, Frances.M. 1988. A critique of the feminist charges against prostitution. *Atlantis* 4(1): 82–89.

Shaver, Frances M. 1993. Prostitution: A female crime? In *Conflict with the law: Women and the Canadian Justice system*, eds. Ellen Adelberg and Claudia Currie, 153–173. Vancouver: Press Gang.

Shaver, Frances M. 1996. Prostitution: On the dark side of the service industry. In *Post critical criminology*, ed. Thomas O'Reilly Fleming, 42–55. Scarborough: Prentice Hall.

Shaver, Frances M. 2005. Sex work research : Methodological and ethical challenges. *Journal of Interpersonal Violence* 20(3): 296–319.

Shaver, Frances M, and Meyer Weinberg. 2002. Outing the stereotypes: A comparison of high track strolls in Montreal, Toronto, and San Francisco. Paper presented at the society for the scientific study of sex, annual meeting, Montreal, Quebec, Canada.

Sherman, Susan, Jacqueline Reuben, Chris Chapman, and Pamela Lilleston. 2011. Risks associated with crack cocaine smoking among exotic dancers in Baltimore, MD. *Journal of Drug and Alcohol Dependency* 114(2–3): 249–252.

Sloan, Lacy, Holly Bell, and Chris Strickling. 1998. Exploiter or exploited: Topless dancers reflect on their experiences. *Affilia: Journal of Women and Social Work* 13(3): 352–368.

Sloan, Lacy, and Stephanie Wahab. 2000. Feminist voices on sex work: Implications for social work. *Affilia* 15: 457–479.

Sloss, Christine, and Gary Harper. 2004. When street sex workers are mothers. *Archives of Sexual Behavior* 33(4): 329–341.

Spittal, Patricia, Julie Bruneau, Kevin Craib, Pamela Miller, Francois Lamothe, Amy Weber, K Li, Mark Tyndall, Michael O'Shaugnessy, Martin Schechter. 2003. Surviving the sex trade: A comparison of HIV risk behaviors among street-involved women in two Canadian cities who inject drugs. *AIDS Care* 15(2): 187–195.

Staiger, Annegret. 2009. The economics of sex trafficking since the legalization of prostitution in Germany in 2002. *The Protection Project: Journal of Human Rights and Civil Society* 2: 103–119.

Stein, Arlene. 2010. Sex, truths, and audiotape: Anonymity and the ethics of exposure in public ethnography. *Journal of Contemporary Ethnography* 39(5): 554–568.

Stella, By and For Sex Workers in Montreal. 2006. Sex workers and research ethics. Montreal: Stella. Accessed from: http://www.chezstella.org/docs/ConsSIDArechEthiA.pdf.

Surratt, Hilary, Steven Kurtz, Jason Weaver, and James Inciardi. 2005. The connections of mental health problems, violent life experiences, and the social milieu of the "stroll" with the HIV risk behaviors of female street sex workers. *Journal of Psychology and Human Sexuality* 17(1/2): 23–44.

Surratt, Hilary, James Inciardi, Steven Kurtz, and Marion Kiley. 2004. Sex work and drug use in a subculture of violence. *Crime and Delinquency* 50: 43–59.

Sweet, Nova, and Richard Tewksbury. 2000. Entry, maintenance and departure from a career in the sex industry: Strippers' experiences of occupational costs and rewards. *Humanity and Society* 24: 136–161.

SWOP/Sex Workers Outreach Project Chicago. How to be an Ally to sex workers. Chicago: SWOP, n.d. Accessed from: http://redlightchicago.wordpress.com/how-to-be-an-ally-to-sex-workers.

Thompson, William E., Jack L. Harred, and Barbara E. Burks. 2003. Managing the stigma of topless dancing: A decade late. *Deviant Behavior* 24: 551–570.

Tolich, Martin. 2010. A critique of current practice: Ten foundational guidelines for autoethnographers. *Qualitative Health Research* 20: 1599–1610.

U.N./United Nations. 2003. Statement by his Excellency Mr. George W. Bush, President of the United States of America, address to the United Nations General Assembly. http://www.un.org/webcast/ga/58/statements/usaeng030923.htm. Accessed 23 Sep 2003

U.S./United States Congress. 2008. Tom Lantos and Henry J. Hyde United States Global Leadership against HIV/AIDS, Tuberculosis, and Malaria Reauthorization Act of 2008. 110th Congress. Accessed from: http://www.pepfar.gov/documents/organization/108294.pdf.

U.S./United States Department Of State. 2012 Trafficking in persons report. Accessed from: http://www.state.gov/j/tip/rls/tiprpt/2012/.

U.S./United States Department Of State. 2006 A Statement On Human Trafficking-Related Language. Accessed from: http://2001-2009.state.gov/g/tip/rls/rm/78383.htm.

U.S./United States Department Of State. 2004. The link between prostitution and sex trafficking. http://2001-2009.state.gov/r/pa/ei/rls/38790.htm. Accessed from 24 Nov 2004.

U.S./United States National Security Presidential Directive. 2003. Trafficking in Persons National Security Presidential Directive. http://www.fas.org/irp/offdocs/nspd/trafpers.html. Accessed from 25 Feb 2003.

Uygun, Banu. 2004. Post-socialist scapes of economy and desire: The case of Turkey. *Focaal: European Journal of Anthropology* 43: 27–45.

Valverde, Mariana. 1987. Too much heat, not enough light. In *Good girls/bad girls: Sex trade workers and feminists face to face*, ed. Laurie Bell, 27–33. Toronto: Women's Press.

Van der Meulen, Emily, and Kara Gillies. 2007. Organizing sex workers. *CriticalTimes* 4(3): 9.

Van der Meulen, Emily, Elya Durisin, and Victoria Love, eds. 2013. *Selling sex: experience, advocacy, and research on sex work in Canada*. Vancouver: University Of British Columbia Press.

Van der Meulen, Emily. 2011. Action research with sex workers: Dismantling barriers, building bridges. *Action Research* 9: 370–384.

Van der Meulen, Emily. 2011b. Participatory and action-oriented dissertations: the challenges and importance of community-engaged graduate research. *The Qualitative Report* 6(5): 1291–1303.

Vanderstaay, Steven. 2005. One hundred dollars and a dead man: Ethical decision making in ethnographic fieldwork. *Journal of Contemporary Ethnography* 34: 371–409.

Vanwesenbeeck, Ine. 2001. Another decade of social scientific work on sex work: A review of research 1990–2000. *Annual Review of Sex Research* 12: 242–287.

Visweswaran, Kamala. 1994. Feminist reflections on deconstructive ethnography. and "Sari Stories". In *Fictions of Feminist Ethnography*. Minneapolis: University of Minnesota Press.

Wahab, Stephanie. 2003. Creating knowledge collaboratively with female sex workers: Insights from a qualitative, feminist, and participatory study. *Qualitative Inquiry* 9(4): 625–642.

Wahab, Stephanie, and Lacy Sloan, 2004. Ethical dilemmas in sex work research. *Research for Sex Work (R4SW 7): Sex Workers Health, HIV/AIDS, Ethical Issues Care and Research* 7: 3–5.

Wallerstein, Nina, and Bonnie Duran. 2003. The conceptual, historical and practice roots of community based participatory research and related participatory traditions. In *Community based participatory research for health*, ed. Meredith Minkler, and Nina Wallerstein, 27–52. San Francisco: Jossey-Bass.

Wang, Caroline, Jennifer Cash, and Lisa Powers. 2000. Who knows the streets as well as the homeless? Promoting personal and community action through photovoice. *Health Promotion Practice* 1(1): 81–89.

Wardlow, Holly. 2004. Anger, economy, and female agency: Problematizing 'Prostitution' and 'Sex Work' among the Huli of Papua New Guinea. *Signs: Journal of Women in Culture and Society* 29(4): 1017–40.

Watson, Lori. 2012. A reply to Weitzer. *Violence Against Women* 18(4): 502–505.

Watters, John, and Patrick Biernacki. 1989. Targeted sampling: Options for the study of hidden populations. *Social Problems* 36(4): 416–430.

Weinkauf, Kate. 2011. 'Yeah, he's my daddy': Linguistic constructions of fictive kinships in a street level sex work community. *Wagadu: Journal of Transnational Women's and Gender Studies* 8: 17–29.

Weitzer, Ronald. 2010a. The mythology of prostitution: Advocacy research and public policy. *Sexuality Research and Social Policy* 7: 5–29.

Weitzer, Ronald. 2010b. The mythology of prostitution: Advocacy research and public policy. *Sexuality Research and Social Policy* 7: 15–29.

Weitzer, Ronald. 2005. Rehashing tired claims about prostitution: A response to Farley and Shapiro. *Violence Against Women* 11(7): 971–977.

Weitzer, Ronald. 2000. *Sex for sale: Prostitution, pornography and the sex industry*. New York: Routledge.

Wesely, Jennifer K. 2003. Where am i going to stop?" Exotic dancing, fluid body boundaries, and effects on identity. *Deviant Behavior* 24: 483–503.

West, Rachel. 1998. U.S. PROStitutes Collective. In *Sex work: Writings by women in the sex industry*, 2nd ed, ed. Frederique Delacoste, and Patricia Alexander, 279–289. Cleis Press: San Francisco.

Williamson, Celia, and Terry Cluse-Tolar. 2002. Pimp-controlled prostitution: Still an integral part of street life. *Violence Against Women* 8: 1074–1092.

Williamson, Celia, and Gail Folaran. 2003. Understanding the experiences of street level prostitutes. *Qualitative Social Work* 2: 271–287.

Whelehan, Patricia. 2001. *An anthropological perspective on prostitution: The world's oldest profession*. Lewiston: The Edwin Mellon Press.

Whittaker, Dawn, and Gram Hart. 1996. Research note: Managing risk: The social organization of indoor sex work. *Sociology of Health and Illness* 18(3): 3399–3414.

Wolf, Margery. 1992. *A thrice told tale: Feminism, postmodernism, and ethnographic responsibility*. Stanford: Stanford University Press.

Women with a Vision. 2011. 'Just a Talking Crime': A policy brief in support of the repeal of Louisiana's Solicitation of a Crime Against Nature (SCAN) Statute. New Orleans: Women with a vision. Accessed from: http://wwav-no.org/wp-content/uploads/Final_PolicyBrief_Tal kingCrime.pdf.

Zheng, Tiantian. 2009a. *Red lights: The lives of sex workers in postsocialist China*. Minneapolis: University of Minnesota Press.

Zheng, Tiantian. 2009b. *Ethnographies of prostitution in contemporary China: Gender relations, HIV/AIDS, and nationalism*. New York: Palgrave Macmillan.

Dexter

Call of the Unknown

CPSIA information can be obtained at www.ICGtesting.com
Printed in the USA
LVOW11s1931070114

368464LV00007B/422/P